D0567345

CONCORD PUBLIC LIBRARY
45 GREEN STREET
CONCORD, NEW HAMPSHIRE 03301

DISCARDED

DISCARDED

but this is my
mother!

but this is my mother!

THE PLIGHT OF OUR ELDERS IN AMERICAN NURSING HOMES

Cynthia Loucks

VanderWyk & Burnham
Acton, Massachusetts

362.1
LOU

Copyright © 2000 by Cynthia Loucks

Published by VanderWyk & Burnham
A Division of Publicom, Inc.
P.O. Box 2789, Acton, Massachusetts 01720

All rights reserved. No part of this book may be reproduced or transmitted in any form or by any means without permission in writing from the publisher, except in the case of brief quotations embodied in critical articles or reviews with appropriate citation. Address correspondence to Permissions, VanderWyk & Burnham, P.O. Box 2789, Acton, MA 01720-6789.

This publication is sold with the understanding that the publisher is not engaged in rendering legal, medical, psychiatric, or other professional services. If expert assistance is required, the services of a competent professional person should be sought.

This book is available for quantity purchases. For information on bulk discounts, call (800) 789-7916 or write to Special Sales at the above address.

Library of Congress Cataloging-in-Publication Data
Loucks, Cynthia
    But this is my mother! : the plight of our elders in American nursing homes / Cynthia Loucks.
        p. cm.
    Includes bibliographical references and index.
    ISBN 1-889242-13-6 (hbk.) — ISBN 1-889242-12-8 (pbk.)
    1. Loucks, June Rose, 1908–1995. 2. Nursing home patients—Indiana—Biography. 3. Aged—Institutional care—Indiana—Biography. 4. Nursing home care—Indiana. 5. Nursing homes—Indiana. I. Title.

RA997 .L68 2000
362.1'6'092—dc21
[B]   00-031488

Cover and interior book design by Bruce Bond, Publicom, Inc.
Photographs on pages v and 236 by David Loucks

FIRST PRINTING
Manufactured in the United States of America
10 9 8 7 6 5 4 3 2 1

For my mother
June Rose Loucks
1908–1995

"While the rose said to the sun,
'I shall ever remember thee,'
her petals fell to the dust."

Acknowledgments

MY MOST HEARTFELT thanks go to all the friends and family who never doubted that I could and would write this book, especially Sandy Pedrick, who has believed in me and encouraged me as a writer ever since high school. Faye Weisler was the first to read excerpts and provide me with unflinching feedback about lapses in style and coherence.

I have been deeply inspired by the generosity, vision, and commitment of the many individuals in the reform movement with whom I have spoken. I am grateful to those few nurses and nurse aides who, despite having to work in conditions that continually undermined them, displayed both skill and genuine compassion—especially Margie. Wherever you are Margie, I hope this book that I promised you I would write finds you.

I am indebted to Dr. William Thomas for connecting me to my publisher, VanderWyk & Burnham. The encouragement and patience of Meredith Rutter buoyed me during the last, seemingly endless months of the project. My editor, Patricia Moore, has made a better writer of me, as well as consistently displaying considerable equanimity and kindness when they were most needed. I must also thank Tara, my cat, and Chloe, my dog, who patiently endured my long hours at the computer but dutifully saw to it that walks and meal times were never missed.

I know that my parents would be pleased and proud that I have written this book. I regret that my aunt, Margaret Darland, did not live to see this book completed. She would have been very proud of me, too. And she was so hoping to see me on Oprah. . . .

Contents

FOREWORD

ALMOST HALF OF US in America will be in a nursing home sometime in our lives. We have every right to expect good care there, and if it comes to it, a death with dignity, yet evidence suggests that this is by no means guaranteed. According to 1998 government reports, over 400,000 of the 1.6 million nursing home residents—25 percent—experienced just the opposite, with most receiving harmful care.

Cynthia Loucks's tale sensitively, subtly, and slowly but surely builds overwhelming evidence of the neglectful care that her mother received in what was considered a respectable nursing home. All the instances of poor care that dominated her mother's nursing home stay were, in fact, preventable. All instances disregarded the Federal Nursing Home Reform Law of 1987, a law enacted specifically to protect nursing home residents from inadequate care. All occurred because of short staffing of certified nursing assistants (CNAs) and of licensed nurses, the latter causing poor CNA supervision. And all caused untold suffering for Cynthia's mother and her family.

How did this happen? Part of the answer lies in the role money plays in the industry. Nursing homes are big business, with revenues of $82.7 billion in 1997. There is a continuous tug of war between the nursing home proprietors who want to drive up profits and the government and families who want to lower or maintain costs. In addition to money issues, the philosophy of care and management of both the multifacility, for-profit chains as well as the individual nursing home may be counterproductive, actually preventing staff from placing residents' needs first.

Yet there is good news on the horizon. An increasing number of pioneering nursing homes are willing to think about new ways to provide individualized care. In these homes, staff are stable and assigned permanently to residents, thus fostering relationships. Residents and nursing assistants alike are empowered to make choices, respect one another, and be advocates for one another.

The National Citizens' Coalition for Nursing Home Reform (NCCNHR) is a 25-year-old nonprofit consumer organization that is working to improve the quality of care and quality of life for long term care residents. NCCNHR brings resident concerns to public policy discussions, seeks enforcement of the standards embodied in the Nursing Home Reform Law of 1987, promotes best practices, supports effective citizen advocacy groups and ombudsman programs, and informs and empowers consumers.

Cynthia Loucks's story is the reason we must work together to bring about change and reform in the nursing home industry. We must be committed to paying nursing homes adequately, holding them accountable for the expenditure of money, and demanding good management. It is all of us who will benefit.

Sarah Greene Burger, Executive Director
National Citizens' Coalition for Nursing Home Reform

AUTHOR'S PREFACE

I BEGAN WRITING this book for very personal reasons not long after my mother passed away in a nursing home. I felt compelled to pay homage to the poignant journey that marked the end of her life. At that time, a part of me, knowing that I could no longer make a difference for my mother, wanted to turn my back on the whole ordeal and try to forget it. But I could not. I was haunted by what I had seen, by what my mother had endured, and by how helpless my family had been to protect her. As time went by and I worked through my emotions in my writing, I came to realize that my mother's story is not significant because it is unique, it is significant because it is typical. Her story, in fact, is the quiet nightmare of thousands of elders who are already in nursing homes and the thousands who are yet to arrive.

I realize now that the staff of my mother's nursing home could not possibly have provided her with the care that she required. There were simply not enough of them with adequate skills who cared enough to meet her needs or the needs of others like her. All of us involved in my mother's life back then were caught in a frightful dance that depleted each of us in a different way. It became a burden nearly too much to bear to see my mother robbed of her dignity and robbed of the security and comfort that could have come from receiving kind and skilled care. My family was not allowed the peace of mind of knowing our mother was safe and in competent hands. Instead, we lived with the constant anxiety of thinking about what we had witnessed while we were present—and what we feared might be happening while we were absent.

The care that elders receive in today's nursing homes ranges widely, from abuse or indifference to genuine compassion. The majority of our elders in nursing homes will receive care that falls far short of what we assume and what we count on. It is my hope that this book will galvanize awareness that the entire American nursing home system *needs* to be transformed, and that it *can* be transformed. I hope also that my mother's story will serve as a guidepost to families who presently have loved ones in nursing homes, to enable them to keep fighting for the good care that they deserve. I hope this story will help others to reach out to their loved ones even when they seem unresponsive. I hope that others will learn from my experience, and at the very least, feel less alone. It is the quality of life for our elders that is at stake.

A recent exposé on central Indiana nursing homes ranked all the facilities in the Indianapolis area (where my mother was) by using a point system. Fewer than 10 points was considered a good score, and more than 26 points was considered poor. My mother's nursing home came out slightly above the middle with 16 points. (Some places had more than 100 points!) Based on this evaluation, my mother's nursing home would be considered a fairly average one. That fact is what scares me the most, and, I hope, will scare you, too, after you read about Mama.

but this is my
mother!

1

IT'S PRETTY BAD

There's a common misunderstanding among all the
human beings who have ever been born on the earth
that the best way to live is to try to avoid pain and
just try to get comfortable.

Pema Chödrön, The Wisdom of No Escape

IT WAS A SATURDAY morning, the day before
Easter, 1993. I was alone in my condominium in Santa
Fe, anticipating a pleasant weekend. The past few
months had been a particularly difficult time in my life,
but the turbulence I had been feeling seemed, at last, to
be giving way. I had just begun to savor the ordinariness
of the day when the shrill ringing of the telephone
pierced my complacency.

It seems odd now that I don't remember all the
details of that day, even though I remember how each
moment felt vivid and protracted in the way things do
when time seems to stand still. My cousin was on the
phone from Indianapolis, calling to tell me that Aunt
Margaret had gone to check on my mother when she
hadn't come out of her room for breakfast. Aunt
Margaret had found Mama slumped on the floor, unable

to talk. Mama had been rushed to the hospital and was presumed to have suffered a stroke.

With that single phone call, I suddenly felt isolated, set apart from the ordinary matters of life. I learned I would feel uncomfortable, as well, trying to relate to people who weren't involved in what was happening. The first hint of this and of how alone I would feel with this whole, often incomprehensible experience came the next day when the hostess didn't understand why I couldn't come to her Easter brunch.

Knowing that Mama was alive was a tremendous relief, but not knowing what condition she was in was terrifying. My cousin told me she would call as soon as they heard anything. Right . . . I called the hospital immediately. The nurse in the emergency room told me that Mama's vital signs were stable, but that she was in very serious condition. I asked to speak to her. The nurse informed me that although my mother was conscious, she couldn't speak with anyone because she was making only unintelligible sounds. I hung up the phone and sat there in stunned silence for a couple of minutes. Forcefully the realization hit me that Mama might not be able to talk, but she could listen! I promptly redialed the emergency room and once more asked to speak to my mother. The nurse again insisted that Mama could not talk. "She can hear, can't she?" I replied. "Please, just hold the phone up to her ear."

I composed myself and spoke to my precious mother as calmly and reassuringly as I could, carefully concealing the anguish I felt. I told her how much I loved her, that she should not worry, that everything was being looked after, that she was safe, and that the doctors and nurses would take care of her—everything I could think of to comfort her. She made a lot of sounds, but I could not make out what she was trying to say. I can't imagine how frustrating it must have been for her, but I know she heard me, I believe she understood me, and I hope she was comforted. One thing she said, though, I was able to understand without a doubt. It came out like "Ah ruv oo." As slurred and blurred as the words were, they were unmistakable to my ears. "I love you" told me she was still here, she hadn't left me. Mama was still reaching out, even in the midst of this, to reassure me.

As I hung up the phone, I thought about Mama being alone when she had the stroke. I agonized over how long she might have been lying there on the floor, unable to call for help. Was it so long that valuable time toward her recovery had been lost? And what had it been like for her? Had she been frightened? What had she thought about? I felt the desperate pain of imagining a loved one suffering alone and being helpless to rescue her, and I shook with sobs.

I discovered there is a limbo quality to the aftermath of a crisis that is characterized by a sense of endless waiting. In the beginning, the first day, the hours that pass while you are waiting for some news, some prognosis, can seem like an eternity of time. Each bit of news leads to more waiting, the waiting that occurs when other people are in control. You stay alert, ready to act, but in fact you are always waiting for other people to act. When a life unravels slowly, the way Mama's did, you are always waiting to see what will happen next, wondering whether there will be more suffering or another crisis, vainly hoping that it will somehow get better, and then waiting, ultimately, for the end to come.

My brothers had chosen to travel at once to Mama's bedside in Indianapolis. They were afraid that she was going to die, and they wanted to be there. I was afraid, too, but for some reason I felt that it was not time for me to go. I listened, as best I could, to my innermost feelings, and I stayed put. I began the waiting ritual: specifically, waiting for someone from the hospital to call and report, waiting to see whether Mama's condition would improve or deteriorate. The first hours after a stroke are a critical time as the brain struggles to regain its equilibrium. As with an earthquake, the extent of the damage and whether there will be aftershocks are not immediately known. It is natural to feel desperate for information at such times, and minutes can begin to seem like hours. I tried to reassure myself that since the nurse I had spoken with promised someone would call if there were any change in Mama's condition or any new information, then not hearing anything must be at least okay.

Still, the temptation to ruminate on the worst presented itself repeatedly. Many years of practicing meditation, however, had taught me that worrying like that is self-indulgent and accomplishes nothing. Mama needed me, and I could choose to focus my attention on me or on her. Sitting on my meditation cushion, I began to repeat Metta phrases for Mama: "Mama, may you be happy. May you be peaceful. May you be safe. May you be free from suffering." Metta is a particular Buddhist meditation practice that involves focusing on and directing wishes of loving kindness, ultimately for all beings in the Universe. These phrases are repeated—not in a rote sort of way but with presence and attention to each word, ardently feeling each wish as it is expressed. I prayed, too. My heart ached with apprehension and sorrow, but for the most part, I was calm, and my mind was clear. I waited.

Slowly the day wore on, as days like this inevitably do. After several hours some of the sense of crisis eased when Mama was moved out of emergency and into a room. No one could say what would happen next. No one could answer my relentless questions about my mother's life and tell me what I so urgently wanted to know. But they promised to keep in touch. . . .

A few times after I had spoken with someone at the hospital and didn't think there would be any more news for a while, I went outside and walked around the hills and arroyo near my home. It was a beautiful, sunny, spring day, with the kind of scintillating blue sky that can make New Mexico feel an arm's length from heaven. It helped to get outside. There was more space out there in which to hold the immensity of events. The walls indoors could quickly start closing in on me. Going outside opened me up again, restored some sense of spaciousness. I wandered around aimlessly, appreciating the brilliant sky and feeling caressed by the warm sun on my skin. I prayed for guidance, for some sign. I scanned the earth as I walked, longing for some message. That inner voice, which everyone hears at some time (and hopes at such times is a hot line to God or some direct representative thereof) said over and over to stay where I was, that it was not time to go to her. I found myself drawn to something lying on the ground. It was a tiny, perfectly white feather. Soon I found another feather, the same size and shape, only this one jet black. I cannot explain it, but this was not a message of death. A sense of balance conveyed itself to me—serious but not heavy.

My brothers seemed put off that I wasn't coming to Indianapolis. I explained that I felt I would know if Mama were going to die, that I didn't feel it, and that I was going to wait until after they had left, in order to provide Mama with a family presence for a longer time. They accepted my decision, if somewhat grudgingly. I didn't tell them about the feathers. Their ways of being, of relating to things, are different from mine. What we did share was our love for our mother.

Over the next few days the vigil continued. Every day I spoke to the nurses on the different shifts to get a report. I had them hold the phone to Mama's ear so that I could reassure her that I loved her, that she would be all right, that I would be coming soon. She vocalized back to me, familiar inflections but unintelligible sounds, except for the unwavering "Ah ruv oo." I wondered if my mother would ever converse with me again, and I refused to accept the enormity of the possibility that she might not.

After a few days the sense of immediate danger waned, but no one was offering much in the way of a hopeful prognosis. The stroke had occurred in the right side of her brain, resulting in paralysis of the left side of her body. The relief that Mama had survived the stroke was overshadowed by the fact that her life was going to be altered in ways that I could not bear to consider. Thankfully, her speech did become more clear, although at first I seemed to be the only one who could tell. One of the first things she said to me was, "It's pretty bad."

So she knew.

2

FROM NOW ON

Here is a test to find whether your mission on earth
is finished: If you're alive, it isn't.
Richard Bach, The Reluctant Messiah

LESS THAN TWO WEEKS later, I flew to
Indianapolis. I got in late at night, so I drove straight to
my friend Sandy's house, where I would be staying. Well,
sort of straight. I somehow got off the interstate and
wound up miles out of my way on a dark and unfamiliar
road before I found my way back to the correct route. So
much for thinking I was in familiar territory and knew
where I was going. The metaphor was not lost on me.

Early the next day, in the midst of the morning
commute, I headed for St. Francis Hospital, located in a
section of Indianapolis in which I had seldom been. I
was anxious to get there, and I was not at all confident
about my course, especially after the previous night's
meanderings. I drove on—mind swirling, deep breathing, mind calming—trying to follow the directions I had
written down from a map at Sandy's. As can sometimes

happen with a map, a point came where it no longer corresponded to the reality of the roadways. I kept going, on instinct and adrenaline by then, and finally I saw the buildings that comprised the hospital complex.

My heart was pounding with impatient anticipation as I tried to find a parking space. Once inside the hospital I rushed through the long corridors, having glanced gratefully at the huge lobby statue of St. Francis, comforting and familiar in this otherwise alien environment. I found Mama's room and flew to her side. Like always, I was filled with joy to see her, as she was for me. She knew me without hesitation. I never doubted she would. She was in the bed nearest the window, and I was glad that she had a window to look out, that she could see the sky, colorless though it was on that overcast, early spring day. She had always liked to look at the sky.

While cheerfully greeting Mama and fussing over her in whatever little ways I could, I gingerly surveyed her condition. Although clear pronunciation had returned, her abilities to track a conversation and to find the right words to express her thoughts were plainly diminished from what they had been before this assault on her brain. Her left side was paralyzed, and she was too weak to bear any weight on her right leg. She could turn her head, but mostly only to the right. Limited this way, with only her right arm able to move, she could not reposition herself. She was entirely dependent on medical personnel to move her body.

The sight of her lying there, pale and white-haired in the white bed, was discomfiting, especially so because of the plastic tube that ran into her nose from an IV stand nearby. I knew the stroke had left Mama unable to swallow, but I thought that she would receive her nourishment intravenously. I hadn't realized it would come through a tube in her nose and that the tube would be present all the time. I didn't like it. It looked awful. It didn't look like it could possibly be comfortable, and it was pressing Mama's nose to one side, making it look crooked.

When I first learned about my mother's inability to eat while I was still in Santa Fe, many thoughts had raced through my mind. Although Mama had never gotten around to signing a living will (it was something she had talked about on several occasions), she had been adamant in her preference not to be kept alive by artificial means if she ever became incapacitated. Was the family supposed to let her go then, let her starve? Was that to be her route out of post-stroke suffering? My eldest brother and I spoke briefly about this when we were talking back and forth between Indianapolis and Santa Fe. He echoed my own sense of ambivalence about not wanting our mother to live on in misery nor wanting her to endure a state of hunger. How could we possibly make such a decision? We all wanted to do what was best for her, and relieving her suffering seemed like it must be the most important thing. Wasn't it? I know in our hearts we didn't want to let her go.

From Santa Fe, I had phoned the neurologist who had examined Mama in the hospital, and I raised my questions with him. He informed me that the feeding tube was not considered life support in Indiana, so it was unlikely that it could be legally withdrawn. He did not explain to me what I understand now—that allowing someone to stop eating who doesn't want to eat because death is drawing near is different from withholding food from someone who is not actively dying but who simply cannot take nourishment by normal means.

Ultimately, though, it was all academic, because once I was with my mother and could see how very alive she was despite her condition, there was no question of doing anything other than making provision for her as she was.

Outside of her physical needs, Mama seemed to be a nonperson to the medical personnel at the hospital. To them she was just a confused, sick old lady—"the stroke in 421A." The fullness of her life, the joys and sorrows, the humor, the family she had always held so dear, the music and poetry that she loved, the word puzzles she enjoyed in her old age, the fantastic cook she was, the part of her that wanted to stay home and the part of her that had such a grand time when she didn't stay home were like echoes that the nurses could not hear. What to them were senseless ramblings were to me rich, multi-faceted jewels reflecting images and events from her long life.

Mama talked a lot while I sat next to her hospital bed. Her consciousness was kaleidoscopic. Her thoughts were no longer confined by the usual restriction of past, present, and future as a linear arrangement of discrete events. The rules of organization that we usually impose on our thoughts before vocalizing them no longer applied. The quality of Mama's remarks ranged from ordinary to neurotic, reminiscent to thoughtful, and insightful to cosmic. From moment to moment I was startled, inspired, and anguished by her utterances. The nurses just called her incoherent.

At times Mama seemed to be in some faraway time and place. She frequently spoke about her parents and other family members, with no distinction between those who were alive and those who had long since gone on ahead. I simply listened, trying to make supportive comments and ask appropriate questions. If she thought she was going to see her Mom and Papa pretty soon, who was I to tell her otherwise?

At one point a pensive mood swept over her, and Mama asked me if there was still anything she had to do. I told her I thought she had done a lot already, but I didn't know if there was more. She seemed to be considering that for a few moments. Then I told her that if it turned out there wasn't more for her to do, it would be good to go with the light.

"What light?" she asked me.

"You'll know when you see it," I told her. "Just go with the light."

"Go with the light. Go with the light." She repeated it quietly to herself a few times.

As she lay confined to her hospital bed, Mama frequently worried about getting to the toilet. She kept saying that she wanted to get up and go to the bathroom. I tried to make light of it, telling her that it was okay just to go where she was. She was pretty dubious about that, so I explained about the catheter—simply as a tube and a plastic bag that would collect the urine—and I reassured her that she would not be wetting the bed. "Let it rip, Mama," I would say. She thought that was funny and would repeat it, "Okay, just let it rip." But soon she would be asking to go to the bathroom again. It took her several days to let go of the toilet idea. Was that dementia? I've known presumably functional people in denial over less.

Mama mentioned several times that someone was going to hit her, and she was obviously frightened about it. I have since learned that such fears are not an unusual symptom of degenerative brain disorders. Sometimes these fears are remnants of unresolved issues from the past, and other times they are simply a product of confusion. When she said it, however, I reacted as though I were *her* mother, responsible for protecting and comforting her. I promised that no one was going to hurt her and prayed that it was a promise I could keep. I worried whether someone at the hospital had behaved menacingly toward her. A lot of the nurses were pulling double shifts, and I did not see how they could deliver quality care at that rate.

Mama's fear and bewilderment were not uncommon for someone who has suffered a stroke. And for a person who has cognitive impairment, these feelings may be more intensified since the impairment renders the person less able to make sense of what is happening. Unfortunately, in the prevailing medical model, attention is focused almost exclusively on physiological conditions, and little attempt is made to address psychological suffering.

Perhaps I should have spoken outright to Mama about the stroke. It never occurred to me to ask her if there was anything she wanted to know. It can be difficult to distinguish between protecting a loved one from unnecessary suffering and meeting her need to understand what is happening. One guideline that is easily adhered to and that I learned later is to follow the person's lead by truthfully answering any questions that are asked. Of course, that guideline does not help if the ability to ask is impaired but the desire to know is not. On the other hand, telling a person something that she does not have the means to cope with is not a kindness. Since there is no formula that fits everyone, each person must be considered individually in order to discover how best to provide assistance. Hospital social workers can be most helpful at these times if they are thoroughly trained in offering guidance to families and patients in the aftermath of cerebral accidents, and in knowing what effect any pre-existing impairments might have on the situation.

I had been making attempts to learn more about Mama's condition, but the nurses couldn't offer much help. I eventually realized that for someone Mama's age, the story is short: she had a stroke that damaged her brain, how you see her is how she is, she might get better but probably not, she might have another stroke or remain like this until something else kills her. The medical personnel seemed to think I should leave it at that, but I could not easily reconcile myself to it.

Finally, the neurologist came by the hospital room to speak with me. He was a kind and solicitous man but rather oblivious to Mama as a person. He kept asking her if she knew who I was. Even though she clearly did recognize me, she couldn't come up with my name or a descriptive word like *daughter,* especially when she was put on the spot like that. He continued to badger her, as though to drive home the point of her incapacity. I watched, frustrated, but not daring to confront his authority. Once again he asked Mama my name, and this time she replied emphatically, "Periwinkle." Ponderously sober, the doctor shook his head, giving me a knowing look, apparently not recognizing Mama's obvious effort to appease him. Because I knew my mother in a way he could not, I concealed my amusement and told him that I believed his leg had been pulled. He cleared his throat and did not respond, possibly not caring to entertain that interpretation or feeling awkward not to have recognized it.

I wish I had been able to express to the neurologist what was so evident to me. Mama was *not* insensible or hopelessly confused. She had understood the question and was frustrated, probably embarrassed, that she could not produce or find the right words. Struggling, she came up with what was clearly both an affectionate name and an attempt to inject some humor into the sober proceedings. I was, after all, her daughter to name as she pleased. The doctor's inability to recognize the intelligence in her response was sad. As though it were not punishment enough to be unable to coordinate speech and thought, the cruelty of denying her awareness was added. I ached at the thought of how alone she must have felt, trying to communicate but not being understood, or worse yet, seeing people shrug off her attempts and sensing that no one was even trying to understand anymore.

Even though Mama was watching him intently and appeared to follow every word he said, for the entirety of his visit the doctor talked to me about Mama in the third person, as though she were not there. It never seemed to occur to most of my mother's doctors and caretakers that just because she couldn't always find and articulate appropriate words didn't mean that she did not comprehend what they were saying. Although I may not have been able to ascertain exactly what my mother's experience was, I am certain that she was there having one. I am also certain that it was no less meaningful than anyone else's experience.

I always felt guilty for participating in these third-person conversations, of which there were many over the next thirty-two months. I would look at Mama and make some attempt to include her, but I never really confronted anyone with the issue. I avoided generating conflict in her presence, not wanting to risk upsetting her or making her feel she was the cause of it. Besides, I was desperate to talk to these people, to ask them questions and try to get some answers—answers they seldom had—before they rushed off to their next patient.

A precedent was set for me in the hospital that persisted throughout Mama's subsequent stay in the nursing home as well. I would always feel torn between the unavoidable need to cooperate with her caretakers, because of the power they held and our dependency on them, and my longing to protect Mama and demand that they respect her existence. So I juggled between standing up for her and letting things be as they were, lest I offend and alienate the staff. Mama would be the one to pay for that. There was always so much, so overwhelmingly much, that disturbed me about how people took care of her. Yet, it was clear from the start that I would have to pick my battles.

As much as I was anxious to shield Mama and spare her anything that I could, I couldn't prevent the nurses from forever quizzing her on such distinctly irrelevant data as the date or the day of the week. The prevailing philosophy in the care of people with brain injuries is to attempt constantly to orient them to the everyday world. Essentially, the medical approach to brain-injured individuals is to try to pull them back into our world via so-called reality orientation rather than try to enter and understand the world in which *they* are existing. For Mama, who was going on eighty-five years old when her stroke occurred and who had been in a gradual process of disengaging from the world for a few years, insisting that she "orient herself to reality" seemed not only foolish but cruel as well. There was little of hope and cheer in her circumstances, so the less she dwelled on them the better. (Recently, when my Aunt Margaret was succumbing to cancer, a cousin told me that our aunt thought she was staying in a bed-and-breakfast inn; it was a notion that Aunt Margaret apparently found quite comforting. "For goodness sake," I urged my cousin, "don't tell her anything different!")

It made me feel bad, and probably did Mama, too, that they kept asking her questions she couldn't answer.

They should have asked her things like who her favorite poet was. I didn't have to ask, of course; I certainly knew, and with a little encouragement she was reciting James Whitcomb Riley poems with me. We had fun, and that alone made it much more worthwhile than identifying the day of the week.

Many times my conversations with Mama ended in frustration for both of us because she was avidly trying to get something across to me, and I could not figure out what it was. She seemed to know what she meant, but she simply could not bring forth the words she needed. What a shock it must be to function at a certain level one moment and then abruptly have a major portion of your communication abilities erased in an instant, in one stroke as it were. (Suddenly, I found the name for this malady chillingly apt.) It seems unfair to expect anyone to deal with such a huge transformation all at once. Yet we are so quick to dismiss as ramblings of senility a person's efforts to grapple with events that we, who have not experienced them, cannot begin to comprehend.

Anticipation of Mama's placement in a nursing home loomed like a dark cloud. I had to focus my attention on the tasks at hand and the decisions to be made while she was still in the hospital. In order for Mama to get along without that plastic tube going into her nose and down her throat, she would have to undergo an operation that would open a hole in her abdomen. A doctor would then insert a gastrointestinal feeding tube, or G-tube.

Once, when I was a nurse aide, I cared for a woman

who had a G-tube. She had lost the ability to take food orally due to throat cancer, which was the result of years of cigarette smoking, a habit that she refused to relinquish even after paying that price. I would bring her the little cans of liquid nutrition, and she would pour them into the tube. She was always particular about what flavor she had, even though she couldn't taste it.

The thought of it all made me queasy. The doctor assured me that once the initial incision healed, it would be painless, and there would be less irritation and chance for infection with the tube on the outside rather than the inside, like the one inserted through her nose. Also, more substantial nutrition could be delivered through the G-tube, since it was much larger. I could not refute such basic issues as avoiding infection and providing adequate nutrition. Although they could not legally install the device without the family's permission, the attitude was one of a foregone conclusion with which I was expected to comply without further ado.

I was naturally anxious about Mama having surgery so soon after her stroke. The surgeon advised me that they had waited these two weeks to be sure she was stable enough for the operation to be reasonably safe. They told me what I needed to hear. I was feeling frightened, helpless, and overwhelmed, to the point of being emotionally numb, as I found myself having to make a decision about which I did not feel well informed. I needed someone to convince me that it was okay. The doctors were eager to oblige. What bothers me now is that no one mentioned that Mama's ability to swallow could return within a few weeks. The doctors wanted to do the surgery right away. They wanted to avoid the cost of another hospitalization if we delayed and Mama had to be returned to the hospital for the operation. Maybe I should have insisted they wait. I didn't.

I knew that my brothers were in favor of the path that promised to make the going easier for Mama. I suspect that they were glad to have left the immediate, stark reality of the situation behind and to have left the final decision in my hands. (It occurs to me that since they refrained from observing the intimate elements of Mama's care, they probably never did see that hole in her abdomen and the plastic tube hanging from it, which I witnessed over and over again during her stay in the nursing home. Aunt Margaret confided in me that she believed they had just slipped the tube into Mama's navel, a much more agreeable notion than thinking they had cut a hole into her sister's abdomen.)

It was a painful decision to make. Mama was so very much alive, still present, despite her physical paralysis and altered mental state. Removing the nasogastric tube and going to a G-tube would represent further medical intervention and a conscious decision to keep Mama alive *despite* our mutual dread of a nursing home. Who was I to say that this form of her life was not valid, should not be? How could I know what meaning the experience might have for her soul, or for mine? These questions parked themselves in my mind and overruled squeamish hesitation. Whatever it all meant, it appeared that it was to be our dharma, our destiny. So with a heavy heart I consented to the operation, signed the paper, and stepped into the river of medical control over my mother's life.

I walked alongside Mama's gurney as she was wheeled to the operating room, reassuring her with more confidence than I felt. Afterwards, I sat with her in the recovery room, anxiously watching the monitor, waiting for her to wake up. I started thinking that it was my fixed attention that kept her vital signs in place. Catching myself, I redirected my thoughts and noticed how depleted I was. I decided to step out for a while. I thought it was the best time to go, since I would not want to leave when she was awake. With assurance from the nurse that Mama was in no immediate danger, I headed for the hospital cafeteria. Somehow, eating while Mama was unconscious was less of a betrayal of her inability to join me in a meal.

The cafeteria was in the basement, in a drab, fluorescent-lit room. I passed by a lot of things I didn't want before I came upon the steaming tray of cauliflower. "I'll take that," I pointed. It took the server a moment to grasp that I just wanted cauliflower. No cheese sauce. Nothing else. She peered at my thin frame and heaped the plate high. There wasn't much attempt at presentation. It was so bland, so monotonously off-white. It kind of faded into the plain, white plate, like so much else in the hospital. As I sprinkled the cauliflower with salt and pepper and watched the steam rise, I suddenly felt cozy in the midst of so much starkness. I still remember how it tasted, that not quite describable taste of cauliflower, and how it sort of squeaked as I chewed it. I savored each bite, feeling thoroughly nourished, grateful to have found a fresh, properly cooked vegetable in that hospital cafeteria. I didn't let myself think about Mama eating.

Eventually, Mama woke up, but she was groggy for a long time, at least twenty-four hours. I hadn't considered that and regretted it very much, given the limited time we had together. Although she came through the surgery just fine from a medical standpoint, I know that it took a lot out of her. Meanwhile, I had another responsibility to attend to.

The bulk of Mama's personal belongings were in a storage compartment at the apartment building where she had lived with Aunt Margaret. My job was to retrieve her things, pack what she needed for life in a nursing home, and figure out what to do with the rest. After spending the days at the hospital, I would spend the evenings going through my mother's belongings, in a way going through her life, discovering the things that she had chosen to save over so many decades.

Sandy kept me company. Mona, another long-time friend, came over and sat with us sometimes, too. It was a comfort to have them there, my oldest friends, to have witnesses, friends to share each awesome discovery with. It seemed like such a short time ago that we were in high school, full of dreams, magnifying every drama. Now here we were in our forties, leading lives we never expected to be leading, reminiscing about our fathers who had all since died, trying to comprehend what had happened to my mother, who was always so *there*, making us something to eat, being concerned, and now being in need of care herself. Her life seemed so reduced. A bed, a room, and some boxes holding the artifacts of her life—was this all that was left?

I felt the enormity of deciding what to do with someone else's things, things that had meant enough to be saved for a lifetime, things that belonged to someone who mattered so very much to me. It seemed important to look at every single item, every card, every nylon stocking, every button in the button tin. If it was worthy enough for Mama to save it, then it deserved at least to be seen, to be attended to individually. And so it went, hour after hour, through hundreds of items of all sorts, dividing it all into piles that designated each thing's fate. There was very little that I could bear to throw out. That just wasn't our family's way.

Besides Mama's pile and those things my brothers had already chosen, there was a pile for Goodwill, two piles of special mementos for Mona and Sandy, a pile for my niece and nephew to take to my sister. I confess I kept the real treasures for myself, like the faded old tin with the rabbits on it that had held—for as long as I could remember, and longer—a vast collection of buttons. I am certain that no button ever went into the trash on Mama's watch. There were hundreds of them, buttons of every size and kind. Sandy helped me sort them. I saved the rare and unusual ones, abalone, for instance, and other styles that hadn't been manufactured in years. But some of the ordinary plastic ones I sent to Goodwill, an irreverence I have since regretted.

One of the most astonishing discoveries was a stack of letters that Mama had saved since the 1930s, when she was in her early twenties and her father was being treated for cancer at the Mayo Clinic in Minnesota. Mom (the name by which all generations referred to my grandmother) had gone to be with him. As soon as I realized what I had found, I carefully packed away the letters, later to be read and savored with great veneration. They have provided a wonderful window into my mother's family. Through them, I got to know a family that loved and struggled and survived. They hold the only words I have ever heard from my grandfather, whom I never met. (He never came home from the clinic. Having survived the surgery, he wound up dying from complications of pneumonia, only a few years before the antibiotics that could have saved his life were widely available.) Other letters reflected the unwavering strength and perseverance of my grandmother, who was left a widow with four children still at home, in the days before Social Security or life insurance existed, let alone good job opportunities for single mothers.

One of the best discoveries was the picture of a rabbit I had drawn in the second grade. It was made on green construction paper, with very long, thin ears and innocent, beseeching eyes. Tears slipped down my cheeks, knowing Mama must have treasured it to have saved it for all these years.

Sometimes the reality of everything threatened to swamp me. I couldn't stand to think about the irrevocability of what was unfolding, that time had signaled such a colossal shift in both Mama's life and mine. So much that had been before would never be again. It wasn't so much that our day-to-day relationship would change— that had been happening for a few years as confusion gradually began to overtake Mama. What hovered in my peripheral awareness was that Mama and I would never again enjoy the intimacy and privacy of home. The knowing of this loss was always there, unspoken, unattended to in the hustle and bustle of dealing with what was happening each moment. From now on Mama would be in the hands of strangers. Our time together, our lives together, would never quite be our own again.

3

The Long and Winding Road

> My memory and my brains have gone to wait for
> me somewhere else.
>
> *Michelangelo*

EVEN THOUGH WE HAD known that Mama was
at risk for stroke, and Mama and I had talked about this
and how awful it would be, we didn't *really* grasp how
really awful it would be. When Mama had her stroke, I
could no longer deny where my mother's life was going.
At the same time, I was confronted with the realization
that I cannot control someone else's life, nor can I possibly know how someone else's life is supposed to go.
After years of thinking that Mama's life could and
should somehow be different, I finally accepted that it
was exactly how it was supposed to be. It was her life,
and not something I was necessarily privy to understand,
much less alter.

The conceit of having control over even my own
life grew increasingly precarious. I was forced to admit
that my life is as much a mystery to me as is anyone

else's. I can read all sorts of meaning into what has already happened. I can construct themes, patterns, intentions, even prognostications, but ultimately, I have no idea what it all adds up to or how it will unfold. With that understanding in mind, I began to face the enormous changes in both my life and my mother's— changes I could choose to cooperate with but could not control.

I pondered how Mama had been transformed from the vital, capable, hard-working woman who had raised me, into the frightfully frail old lady whose bed I was to spend so many hours sitting beside. It troubled me that she was in the custody of strangers, people who had never met the younger Mama. I was afraid that, by not knowing anything about her life, they would somehow erase her identity. I wanted to show them pictures and tell them stories, but it was clear that they didn't have the time and weren't really interested. All that would ever be real to the nurses and the aides was Mama in her present condition, an often cheerful but sometimes frightened, cranky, confused old lady. I eventually became resigned to their perceptions, this done more easily once I realized that the whole of Mama's life was not lost so long as I held those memories. So while I privately cherished who she had been and remembered who was lying there so helplessly, I learned to think of the situation as one of change more than loss. Besides, Mama was the most beautiful old lady I had ever seen.

My mother was named June Rose, and she had all the delicacy, strength, and beauty the name implies. She was a lady, genteel, gracious, proud, and modest, a person of dignity and deportment. She was caring, exacting, and funny. I thought of her thick, wavy, auburn hair that she had always been so proud of and how stunning she looked in colors like turquoise and teal. I treasured her old-fashioned jewelry, collected since her adolescence, and the memory of how we used to sit on the bed and spread out the jewelry as she told me stories about each piece. I reflected on her kindness, her sense of humor, her shyness, her meticulous housekeeping, and on how good everything she cooked always tasted.

It occurred to me how much we identify people by what they love. In Mama's case it was trees, especially in their autumn finery; hummingbirds; Riley's poems such as "Out to Old Aunt Mary's" and "The Raggedy Man"; heartfelt melodies like "Lara's Theme" (from *Dr. Zhivago)* and "Greensleeves." Mama loved beauty, whether it was wrought in the form of a gorgeous sunset or a finely crafted piece of furniture. Sometimes I felt sad that so much of that appreciation had dropped away, and yet it seemed okay, too. We all must eventually leave behind the things of the world, whether slowly, like Mama did, or all at once. What remained for Mama, though, was a large measure of graciousness and friendliness, and an unwavering recognition of love.

Disorientation and loss of short-term memory had been creeping up on Mama for many years. I have tried to recall when the unraveling began, but I cannot pinpoint it. I remember when Mama was as sharp as a tack and also when she was uncertain as to what had happened a few hours ago. But the change was so gradual, the increments so subtle, that no distinct turning point was apparent.

When Mama came to visit me in California in 1977, it was the first time we had ever been completely on our own together, and we had a grand time. She was almost seventy years old by then. The sight of her, with her pants legs rolled up, strolling along the beach in her bare feet, was such a delight. In that dawn of my adult relationship with her, I got to know a playful, light-hearted side of my mother. I thought Mama was all right then and still okay when she visited me again in 1979, several months after my father's death. But now, when I reflect upon it, I am not so sure. There were little things, moments of disconnect, not the sort of things one would normally give a second thought to, unrecognized fore-runners of what was to come.

Within the next few years Mama began to com-plain frequently about her memory. I didn't really think much about it. For one thing, I didn't see as much evi-dence of it as Mama was undoubtedly experiencing. I also didn't know any better than to take for granted that people in their seventies have memory lapses, and so I dismissed her complaints and the possibility of under-lying problems. Nothing had prepared me to see my mother get old, to see her lose ground. I didn't want to believe it might be happening or to face the helplessness that I would one day have to come to terms with.

Eventually, it was undeniable that something was awry with Mama. She seemed increasingly anxious and got confused and sometimes irritable about relatively simple things. Her expressions of concern about her memory grew ever more frequent, while her family proceeded to make the typical mistakes that families make at these times. We tried to reason with her, or to explain things *ad nauseum,* as though we could coerce her brain into functioning properly, as though her will had something to do with it. Most families, including my own at the time, don't recognize the connection between memory loss and the subsequent behavioral and emotional changes that can occur, and are quite ignorant of how to handle them or how to provide effective support for the person going through these changes. I feel such remorse for this now, knowing that we could at least have eased her distress if we had understood more about what was happening and how to respond appropriately. I was so relieved when a doctor said Mama did not have Alzheimer's. The connection that I didn't make, however, and that the doctor didn't make for me, was that the conditions were similar enough that we could have benefited enormously from information about how to care for someone with Alzheimer's.

Many times when Mama went to see a doctor, she reported her difficulties with memory loss and confusion as well as "odd" sensations she often experienced in her forehead. Not one of the doctors ever offered her any real help. Unfortunately, this seems to be the rule, not the exception. Elders complaining of memory loss, confusion, and other such symptoms, who go to physicians and are given the dispiriting diagnosis of "dementia," are often sent away ill-provided with regard to guidance or resources for understanding and dealing with their situation. At best, they might get a prescription for a blood-thinning medication if their physical condition signals they are at risk for stroke. There are widespread complaints that doctors typically do not put patients or their families in touch with organizations or individuals who might provide nonmedical information and support.

The medical diagnosis for my mother's condition was multi-infarct dementia. Over the years she apparently had suffered numerous small strokes, known as TIAs, transient ischemic attacks, each taking its toll on her brain. With each attack, her capillaries filled with scar tissue, which impeded the flow of blood, with its cell-sustaining oxygen, to her brain. I deeply regret that we did not seek out more information about Mama's condition. I know that it was frightening for her to feel herself losing ground mentally. As is so often the case, no one close to her really knew how to help, much as we wanted to. And like many people in similar situations, I didn't know how much I didn't know, and I never thought to ask the doctor for further assistance or to find out whether other resources and help might be available. In addition, I was almost entirely oriented toward preventing more deterioration and not toward handling the existing deterioration.

In truth, I do not really know what, if anything, might have stemmed the course of Mama's decline and changed the direction of her final years. The arrogance that once enabled me to believe that I knew what was best for her, that I could possibly know how her life ought to unfold, has long since been dispelled. I do know that given the proper information and tools, we could have better understood and assisted her in what she was going through.

We tried to keep her spirits up by joking about it, as though Mama's forgetfulness were a comic routine. She wrote me once that she didn't really like being the object of jokes, but that it was worth it to bring laughter to her family. One of her greatest frustrations in life was feeling that she didn't convey to her family the love she felt for us. I remember her ruing the fact that she wasn't "demonstrative," as she called it. I was pleased to be able to reassure her that, with me, she was doing quite a good job of conveying her love. Besides telling me all the time, she wrote me loving letters, while she still could, always offering encouragement, expressing faith in me, and supporting whatever I was doing in my life.

There was a mercifully brief, rather discordant period when Mama was given to directing some very sharp remarks at me. At the time, I didn't know what to make of it and was quite disturbed. Now, I see it as part of her illness and recognize the irony in it. I have no doubt that I was the person she could most trust to neither abandon her nor lash out at her, and that made me the safest outlet for her frustration and anger.

If anything, Mama's forgetfulness deepened my awareness of how profoundly connected we were, because she clearly always recognized me as someone she loved, even if she didn't have a fix on the details of our relationship. She went through a phase a couple of years before the stroke when she insisted on calling me "Ruth," which was the name of her youngest sister, who had died a few years earlier. I don't look anything remotely like Aunt Ruth, who had black curly hair, brown eyes, and olive skin; I am fair skinned, with honey-colored hair and green eyes. Once, in exasperation at my inability to convince Mama that I was not Ruth, I got out a photo album and triumphantly pointed to a picture of Aunt Ruth, certain that she would now make the distinction. "Who is that?" I asked. "You," Mama replied, without hesitation. It never occurred to me just to be Ruth and let Mama work out whatever that was all about, but I did stop correcting her.

There was sometimes a very dear, childlike quality to Mama's forgetfulness. Everything was fresh and new to her, something to delight in. You didn't need a big repertoire of jokes with her in those days. You could tell the same joke every second day or so and get the same hearty laugh. Once I brought my Walkman on a visit. I inserted one of her favorite musical pieces, the soundtrack from *My Fair Lady,* and put the headphones over her ears. She was a little perplexed that I couldn't hear it, too, and dubious about the value of that, but she was delightfully intrigued that she could take the music wherever she went. She then proceeded to march all around the house while it played.

Being able to enjoy Mama throughout her life is something for which I will always be thankful. This is not to say that I didn't also experience dismay and frustration at times, especially when Mama was distressed in some way, and my clumsy, ill-informed efforts were only making the situation worse. One of the things I learned the hard way is that you never tell a disoriented person about an appointment ahead of time. Since the person can no longer track time, she is likely to obsess and will constantly ask if it is time to go, or will get ready hours or even days ahead of schedule. I should have been much more suspicious of Mama's mental state at the end of a family gathering in Colorado, more than a year before we realized Mama could no longer live on her own. The day we were all to leave, Mama got up at 3 A.M. to start packing. We both got pretty frazzled as I tried to convince her to shut off the light in our motel room and go back to sleep until morning.

Mama felt very strongly about her independence and had always asserted that she had no intention of ever moving in with any of her children. All of us respected that choice and so joined her in resisting the inevitability of her loss of autonomy. For a while Mama lived in the same apartment building as one of her sisters, Bert. But when Aunt Bert died, Mama moved into an apartment complex for seniors, where there were group meals and daily apartment checks to ensure each resident was okay. We hoped this would work for her, and frankly we didn't consider what might lie ahead. She was satisfied with the arrangement, and that was good enough.

Occasionally Mama would get the notion to go to a nearby store, but upon returning to the complex of identical multistory buildings with identical rows of apartments, she could not figure out which one was hers. Someone would eventually notify the superintendent, who would fetch her and return her to her place. He soon became exasperated with this chore and insisted that she could not continue to live there.

Because my siblings and I all lived in different

parts of the country, having the family, as a group, care
for Mama was not an option. We discovered, too, that it
was futile trying to care for her individually. Mama
wound up spending more than two years literally being
passed from one family home to another, where invariably no one had the ability or the resources to care for
someone in her condition and everyone got completely
stressed out trying.

For a time while she was living with her youngest
son, Mama was able to attend a senior day-care program. I visited her there one morning and found her
glowing with pleasure, playing games and singing songs
with the other folks. That was the first time it ever
crossed my mind that, despite all my trepidations about
nursing homes, maybe Mama would be better off in the
hands of professionals than with her well-meaning but
essentially ill-equipped relatives. Mama and I actually
visited one California assisted-living facility together.
The level of activity and care for people in a similar condition to Mama looked very promising. However, I
knew that the unfamiliarity and absence of family would
have been difficult for her at that stage. In any case, mine
is not a family that has cultivated the ability to sit down
together and make decisions, so the pattern of passing
Mama from one relative to another continued.
Meanwhile, looking after her didn't get any easier.

Ironically, although I seemed to be the one who
had the most patience with Mama in her confusion, I
was not in a good position to have her with me. In due
course, she took a turn at coming to stay with me in
Santa Fe, but it was a temporary arrangement from the

start, covering the time period between when the coping limit had been reached in one home and when another home was ready for her.

I found the logistics of having Mama live with me very difficult. I had concerns about leaving her alone in the house. I looked into senior day-care programs in my area and found that, even with their sliding scale, the minimum cost per day—a short day, not a business day—was so high that sending her even once a week could be a strain on a tight budget. Fortunately, I was working somewhat curtailed hours at the time, and my office was only five minutes away, so I was able to avoid leaving Mama alone for long periods of time. I taped a large sign to the front door to remind her that I would be home soon and to please not go out until I returned. There was a nice, big, enclosed back yard where she could go, and she busied herself with letting the cat and dog in and out. They, of course, took full advantage of her willingness to provide that service.

Even when I was right there, Mama was often confused as to where she was. All the moving around had really pulled the rug out from under her. A home-body like Mama just couldn't get her bearings with so many changes of residence. I wrote down information that I thought she would find reassuring, including that she was at my house in Santa Fe. I especially hoped this written list would help her when she awoke in the middle of the night and didn't know where she was. Alas, she usually did not remember to read it.

Mama wanted so much to be a help in some way, but her efforts in the kitchen did not go very well. She loaded and unloaded the dishwasher diligently, but never noticed whether the dishes were clean or dirty! Finally, I found a job for her that she enjoyed immensely. A row of hibiscus bushes all along the back of the house were in full bloom. She took great pleasure in going out each day and plucking off any wilted blossoms. I was touched by how important it was to her to feel useful.

By the time Mama was with me in Santa Fe, I had learned to stay in the present with her and to find connection where I could. She enjoyed going with me for short walks around the neighborhood in the evenings, and then, after she was ready for bed, we would sit and talk for a while. We could still laugh and have a good time together. That was worth a lot.

One beautiful autumn day I took Mama for a ride up into the mountains to the aspen groves to see the trees, golden against the piercingly blue New Mexico sky. This is the sort of thing that Mama, for most of her life, would have considered the height of pleasure. That time, however, I could tell she hardly noticed the scenery, which disappointed me terribly. I had so wanted to do something for her, but all she could do the whole time was question me about where she was going. In painful hindsight I realize how frightening the loss of control over her life must have been, how many times by then she had been put into a car and taken someplace, never to return to the starting point. I can barely imagine the disorientation and anxiety she must have felt being in a car—not only not knowing where she was going but also not remembering from where she had set out.

We stopped at a grocery store on the way home. I

left Mama in the car, securely fastened in her seat belt, and hurried in to get a couple of items. When I returned, she was nowhere in sight, but the seat belt was still fastened! I stared, disbelieving. How had she gotten out? I ran back into the grocery, thinking she must have come in after me. It was a small store, so I could quickly check all the aisles, but there was no sign of Mama. My god, I thought, she's headed up the street somewhere.

In my panic I kept thinking idiotically, how will I ever explain to the rest of the family that I have lost Mama? I ran out to the sidewalk and looked up and down the street. I could see quite a ways in both directions, but there was still no sign of her. Somewhat relieved, thinking she could not possibly have gotten far enough to be out of sight, I ran back to the parking lot, asking everyone I saw if they had seen her. I ran around to the back of the store, looking everywhere outside. Not knowing what else to do, I went back into the store and looked down all the aisles again. Finally, one of the clerks told me she had seen an elderly woman go into the bathroom. Of course! Where else? But Mama never did disclose how she escaped that seat belt.

The last time I was with Mama, before the hospital and the nursing home, was in Ojai, California, where she lived for a time with one of my brothers. This was just before she returned to Indianapolis to live with her sister Margaret for the last few months before the stroke. Ojai is a beautiful town, and Mama liked it there very much. One last time, we walked together on the beach. Then I took Mama to a restaurant for a slice of lemon meringue pie, her favorite. Before we ordered, Mama went to the restroom. She had been gone several minutes, long enough that I was beginning to wonder. I decided to wait a couple more minutes to give her a chance to manage on her own. It was a good thing I did, because otherwise, I might not have seen her walking briskly down the sidewalk in front of the restaurant. I dashed after her and casually invited her to return with me for a piece of pie. I hope such times that I remember so tenderly and with such gentle humor were not too painful for Mama.

4
NO TURNING BACK

But though my wing is closely bound,
My heart's at liberty;
My prison walls cannot control
The flight, the freedom of the soul.
Jeanne Guyon, "A Prisoner's Song"

AT THE DAWN OF the twenty-first century, stroke remains one of the leading causes of death and disability in the United States. Every year thousands of elders and their families go through the ordeal that attends a disabling stroke, and many victims are admitted to nursing homes. Other diagnoses that put people in nursing homes include such chronic, disabling conditions as Alzheimer's (and other brain disorders), arthritis, and injuries compounded by osteoporosis. In addition, any elder who reaches the point where confusion and difficulties with the tasks of daily living are occurring routinely will likely be considered a candidate for institutionalization. Most of these disabling conditions involve gradual onset, which theoretically allows individuals and their families time to plan ahead for the day when round-the-clock, skilled nursing care may be needed.

Unfortunately, such planning is seldom undertaken—for any number of reasons.

Most seniors clearly hope that whatever ails them will not progress to the point where they can no longer care for themselves, a sentiment shared by their families. Many seniors openly express the desire to die before such an eventuality occurs. Many have strong feelings about not wanting to become a burden to anyone; they have even stronger feelings about losing their independence. They typically think of nursing homes as places where people go to die, a perception that is generally all too accurate, despite widespread denial and minimization of this point by advocates for nursing homes. While it is true that some of the people admitted to nursing homes are there for short-term rehabilitation following a fracture, stroke, or other acute medical problem, the majority are there with a chronic or worsening condition for the remainder of their lives.

I believe that family members, too, often hope, if not openly, that their elders will die before having to go through any major upheaval, including admittance to a nursing home. With no regard for such preferences, life often delivers a moment when the parent—whom the family has always relied on and looked to for care and support—is suddenly the one depending on the family. Some think of this as role reversal, feeling that they have become the parent of their parent. Certainly, it can seem that way when one is making logistical, financial, and health care decisions for a mother or father every day.

Despite their concern, family members are sometimes in the worst position to help. For one thing, the tendency to play down the importance of symptoms is rampant. No one wants to believe that a loved one is growing feeble, much less losing his or her faculties. So families naturally put off making difficult and painful choices for as long as possible. When the time comes to decide whether someone should leave their home, this tendency to put off the decision is reinforced by the negative light in which such a move is usually regarded by the elder. It often takes some dramatic event or someone outside the family calling attention to certain situations before relatives realize the extent of what is happening. Nowadays, too, many grown children live far away from their parents, which means that visits are intermittent and some of the daily problems that an older person might be dealing with go unnoticed.

Another reason planning is delayed for round-the-clock, skilled nursing care is that many families have unrealistic expectations about their own ability to care for their elders. When these expectations are coupled with a devotion that exceeds capacity, the families simply are not prepared when their loved ones' needs go beyond their resources to provide. For individuals, or even families, to provide the degree of care that a completely dependent and impaired person needs is a daunting task. I have seen families determined to keep an elder at home because they feel it is their duty to do so and because they dread the fate they believe awaits the person in a nursing home. Yet I have also seen the subsequent suffering of the elder and the guilt of the family members when the family is no longer able to maintain care at an optimum or even satisfactory level. I have seen, as well, the great personal cost to the caregivers when the demands of home care become so overwhelming as to leave them unable to maintain any outside lives of their own.

Not long ago I visited the home of a middle-aged woman who was caring for her mother who suffered from Alzheimer's. Her mother was at the stage of complete immobility and was barely responsive to speech or other stimuli. She was fastidiously clean, her long, gray-brown hair carefully combed and plaited, and she wore an attractive and spotless flannel gown. I was especially impressed by the sheen of her skin, showing the results of gentle bathings and tender moisture-lotion massages. She had no sores, no bruises.

The daughter worked full-time, and out of her meager salary she managed to pay a home health aide to come in for a few hours per week. The rest of the time, which was twenty-four hours a day, seven days a week (minus the fifteen hours or so she had the aide), the daughter was on her own. Every day, she spent her lunch hour driving almost forty minutes round trip to feed her mother lunch. She also got up several times during the night to turn and tend to her mother, despite having to work the next morning. Although there were several relatives living in the vicinity, they all felt they had too much going on in their own lives to offer any respite, except on the rarest occasions. I was deeply touched by the sight of that fading old lady because she was the most outstandingly well cared for dependent elder I had ever seen.

However, the cost for giving such tender physical care was a daughter who had been left by her husband, who was cut off from friends and any semblance of a life of her own, and who was gradually succumbing to exhaustion. She had an increasingly long list of physical ailments, several of which required serious medical intervention. While her devotion was exemplary, I wondered whether anyone should have to make that sort of sacrifice. Trading the well-being of one person for another is surely not the answer. As a society, we have the resources to care for one another without the cost to any one person ever being as high as it was for that daughter. These resources need to be used wisely, not only to help caregivers but also to help our elders who presently languish in nursing homes that are ruled by indifference and inadequacy.

Taking care of someone who is both physically impaired and suffering a loss of mental ability is far more difficult than many people realize. Few people have the patience, especially without specialized training, to be constantly around a person who is disoriented and confused. The literature abounds with examples of unkind and inappropriate, even abusive, behavior directed at these hapless sufferers by their overwhelmed caregivers. While such behaviors may be understandable, they are certainly not acceptable. People who cannot control their behavior due to illness need to be treated compassionately and should never be punished for what they cannot help. Caretakers who lose control have no business continuing to "care" for someone in their homes.

While home care of elders by loving relatives may remain the ideal, many families relinquish a relative to an institution because they can no longer provide adequate care themselves. They are motivated by the belief that their loved one will receive a higher quality of care in the hands of the professionals than is possible at home. Families imagine they will be relieved of, to some great degree, the role of caretaker. For the lucky ones who find an excellent placement for their relative, this is indeed the case. For most, however, it is far from it. The way the majority of nursing homes are run now, we are seldom doing our loved ones a favor by admitting them into these facilities.

The cold reality is that many families find themselves with no other viable choice. Placing a loved one in a nursing home is a choice made typically in the midst of high-pressure circumstances. Whether it is a hospital pressing for discharge after a stroke or accident, a living situation that is no longer safe, or stress levels at the breaking point among over-extended caregivers, the transition to a nursing home is often forced to take place abruptly, with as little as a few days to prepare.

For family members, this can be an intensely emotional time. They are beginning to experience grief over the loss of a functioning parent, spouse, or other close relation. They are assaulted by feelings of frustration and helplessness because they realize there is so little they can do to help. They are besieged by guilt about placing a loved one in the care of strangers. Sometimes these feelings are accompanied by anger at being put in the position to have to make such decisions about someone's life. All these feelings can precipitate tension, conflict, anxiety, digestive disorders, depression, insomnia, and other upsets. The person who is being placed in the nursing home is often feeling disoriented, frightened, despairing, and angry. Exhaustion is common for all concerned at this stage.

It is at this point, with a family's psychological, emotional, and physical resources stretched to the maximum, that family members often find themselves wading through reams of paperwork involving admission and financial data while trying to evaluate and somehow choose the most suitable nursing home in their region. In short, it is an exceedingly difficult time when most people urgently want to believe any good news that someone offers them. They usually have precious little wherewithal to question and investigate what they are hearing; they need to believe that they can rely on the people into whose care they are entrusting their loved one. In addition, anticipating the loss of control they will soon have over their loved one's life, family members are eager to forge a positive relationship with the nursing home representatives who will, from now on and in some way, be between them and their loved one.

Much has been written and promoted in the media about how to select a nursing home. These guidelines can be helpful—but only up to a point. Making a valid assessment of a nursing home is difficult when much of what happens, good or bad, within a facility remains hidden until one is in the midst of the nursing home experience. Bruce Vladeck, program administrator for both Medicare and Medicaid during the Clinton administration, wrote in *Unloving Care*:

> Consumers are poorly equipped to evaluate the quality of health care or nursing home services. The 50 percent of nursing home residents adjudged senile may be assumed to be undiscriminating consumers. Families and friends don't do much better; nursing home services are complex, and decisions about nursing home placement are often made under traumatic stress.
>
> Moreover, the quality of health and social services varies, often in unpredictable ways. The third floor of Harry's nursing home may run like a clock with one particular charge nurse and then go to pieces on the night shift, or when the particular nurse retires. A qualitative evaluation made at any one time may only be accurate for that time, yet decisions to "consume" services generally involve long-term commitments.

Most people are limited to selecting a facility within a relatively small geographical area. It is ill-advised, however, to make location the primary factor when choosing a nursing home. Obviously, family members find it more convenient if the drive is a few minutes rather than an hour or more, but it is well worth the extra miles to place a loved one in a facility where the care will be much better. The savings—in heartache for the family struggling with a poor nursing home, and in suffering for the elder living there—surely more than make up for the extra driving time.

Another consideration to keep in mind when choosing among nursing homes is the value of keeping loved ones in their own communities. Even if they do not have personal acquaintances there, being among people of similar ethnic and cultural backgrounds lessens the potential sense of estrangement.

Families are additionally limited in their choices by bed availability and by access to funds. Those who have ample private funds can usually obtain better care than those who do not, but this is not a steadfast rule. The most expensive nursing homes can have the same problems as the less expensive ones have. Not all nursing homes accept Medicaid patients, and in some areas this can put the best-run nursing homes out of many people's reach.

Ultimately, the quality of the care provided by the nursing home is the most important consideration. In any given locality, however, quality of care is very much affected by the regulatory agencies and whether they do their jobs conscientiously or, in the worst cases, look the other way. For this reason, there are regions of the country, and even whole states, that have earned a reputation for having unusually good nursing homes or for having unusually bad ones. Knowing the reputation of a particular nursing home is a good place to start, but there is no substitute for careful inspection and evaluation of the facility. It is a lucky family that finds itself needing a nursing home in an area where one of the better ones can be found. For the less fortunate, the choice may be between bad and worse.

Once the nursing home is chosen, it is important to prepare the elder for this monumental life change. Unfortunately, the more disoriented and disabled the elder is, the less effort is likely to go into such preparation. Both family and medical personnel often make the mistake of thinking that a disoriented person can't understand what is going on. Whether or not the information will be fully comprehended, everyone deserves the courtesy and respect of being given some explanation as to what is happening to them. There are ways to buffer this major transition that are appropriate to each individual, and help should be sought in finding them.

For most individuals and their families, once a nursing home placement has occurred, there is no turning back. Some families may just hope for the best and make the choice with little foundation, thinking that if things don't work out, they can move their relative elsewhere. This is not a good plan, however, because moving old, frail people around can take a tremendous toll on them. It is also a mistake to yield to resignation, thinking that all nursing homes are alike. They are not. Although the clean appearance of the residents and the absence of bad odors are strong positive factors, I learned the hard way that these are no guarantees of the quality of care.

We make all kinds of important decisions in our lives all the time, and few of us have the time or energy to research each choice thoroughly. We get a recommendation here, a caveat there, and then we just pick, because we've got to move on to the next thing. There is no denying that the consumer has the responsibility of selecting the nursing home, but the burden on the consumer would be much more manageable than it is now if nursing homes in general were the kind of nurturing, high-quality places they could be.

In the sometimes overwhelming process of dealing with the physical needs of a frail or disabled loved one, we all too easily forget the emotional and psychological needs of the person who is at the center of it all. This oversight is part of what allows nursing homes and those who depend on their services to be approached as commodities rather than as participants in a mutually interdependent relationship. Restoring people's humanity to the equation of products and services would go a long way toward reforming the system. After all, it isn't the number of beds in a facility that matters so much as the people who are in those beds.

5
REWEAVING OLD THREADS

when past and future dissolve
there is only you
senseless as a lute
upon the breast of God
Rumi

THE HOSPITAL WAS anxious to discharge Mama. Paralyzed on her left side, unable to walk, eat, or provide for any of her own needs, she could not return to the apartment she had been sharing with her sister Margaret. The day that we all dreaded and hoped would never come was upon us. Mama would have to go live in a skilled nursing facility—a nursing home. Although every family member would have liked Mama to be close to them, in her condition it would have been virtually impossible to transport her by commercial airline, much less by car. Mama could not travel to be near any of her children. She would need to go to a nursing home in the Indianapolis area.

I had worked in nursing homes myself, but I was still ill-equipped to be a discriminating consumer when it came to putting my mother into one. Like anyone else,

I didn't know how to tell from the outside what really happened on the inside. I knew that my brother shared my concerns, so when he said that the nursing home he chose was the cleanest facility, and that all the others he had looked at seemed distinctly worse, I accepted that this was the best we could do within the geographical and economic limitations at hand.

I wanted to believe that it was a good nursing home, even though I thought the concept was probably an oxymoron. In any case, with so much that needed attending to, I admit I was glad enough to have someone else deal with selecting the facility. Doing everything by committee was more than my family could manage, so we opted for a division of labor. Without it ever being formally discussed, as I suspect is often the case in other families, it came to be that one of my brothers handled all of Mama's financial affairs and the dealings with Medicare and Medicaid, while I served as her primary medical and personal guardian. In addition, the whole family expressed interest in her care and provided support in whatever ways they could.

Thus, arrangements were made for Mama to be admitted to a reputedly well-regarded nursing home just a few miles from where Aunt Margaret lived. The location, though, brought with it its own limitations. Since none of Mama's children lived in the area, it fell to her sister Margaret to visit the nursing home and keep a watchful eye as best she could. Bless her heart, Aunt Margaret visited nearly every day throughout the time Mama was there. These constant visits must have taken their toll on Aunt Margaret in stress alone. Like many older people, she was overwhelmed by modern traffic and could not manage driving more than a few miles from her home, and not even that when the roads were icy.

Trying to keep at bay the agony and guilt of institutionalizing my own mother, I numbly followed the path of this apparently choiceless choice. The day Mama was moved to the nursing home felt like a nightmare that I couldn't wake up from. There were many more grim days to come, and yet, ironically, some of the moments that touched me most were still to come as well. I kept trying to reassure Mama that it would be okay, that it was a good place, that they would take good care of her there. I don't know if I was very convincing. I felt that Mama, too, sensed the irrevocability of it all. We just bore up, I guess. We did what we had to do.

I felt frantic following her in the ambulance, as though if the ambulance got out of my sight I would somehow never see her again. Entering the facility was an emotional blur. I was directed at once to a small room off the lobby to confront the stack of papers they had waiting for me. The administrative assistant was an amiable young woman who was full of assurances but apparently oblivious to the anxiety that I thought must be emanating from me in thick waves. I sat for a moment and caught my breath, surveying the nicely appointed but windowless office that felt like a respite in purgatory.

Soon I was reunited with Mama in her room. I don't remember much about the room except that Mama's bed was by the window and the natural light made it seem a little more cheerful than it might have seemed otherwise. There was a dresser, a night stand, some shelves, and a closet where I arranged her belongings. I remember wondering how a room could look so inoffensive, so normal, yet still feel so alien.

In the adjacent bed a woman was hooked up to an IV. She, too, had suffered a stroke and was in much worse shape than Mama. She couldn't talk at all, just moaned a little, but I went over and looked into her eyes and talked to her for a while anyway. The woman's daughter came in to visit. She was angry and frustrated with the nursing home and was in the midst of a disagreement about some aspect of her mother's care. I listened to her and tried to offer suggestions as to how she might deal with the situation. I maintained an incredible wall of denial that what she was saying could possibly have any implications for what lay ahead for me and Mama. Even so, a small voice, confined to a little room in my mind, was saying, "Uh oh."

I was glad when she left so I could direct all my attention toward Mama. I undoubtedly prattled a bit; I always do when I'm nervous. Yet, I also remember Mama and me just sitting there quietly—she was in a wheelchair, and I sat in a metal and vinyl chair next to her. Waiting. We spent a lot of the rest of her life waiting together. In a quiet moment, left to my own thoughts, my cheerleader demeanor soon evaporated. I sank into despondency at the thought that I would have to leave Mama in this unfamiliar environment, in the care of yet another set of strangers. I looked up at her, or maybe she looked at me. Anyway, our eyes met. She looked crestfallen as she said, "I wish I were the kind of person that when somebody looks at me their face would light up."

"Oh, Mama," I told her, "you are that kind of person. I was just thinking about something." I can absolutely promise you that I never looked at her again without "lighting up."

After a while a nurse and some aides came in. I had been after them to come and lay Mama in her bed. I knew she was tired, and I didn't want her to have to sit in the wheelchair for so long. As was to be the pattern from then on, it took a long time to get that or any other task accomplished. The nurse was a short, wiry woman, probably close to retirement. Briskly, without so much as introducing herself to Mama, much less explaining what she was doing, she began to examine Mama while she questioned me about her condition. Although I told her that Mama had sustained a stroke and was paralyzed on her left side, this nurse seemed to need to prove it. She began touching Mama in various ways in an attempt to elicit a response. Hoping she would soon satisfy herself, I did not intervene. Since Mama wasn't reacting, and I was pretty numb myself by then, I did not protest when the nurse proceeded to pinch Mama all along her left leg and arm; it seemed it wasn't inflicting physical pain.

I did not anticipate what happened next. Mama looked at me wild-eyed and said, "You've got to get me out of here. They're pinching me!" Horrified, I hastily reassured her, trying to explain what the nurse had been doing. I felt devastated that I had let this happen and alarmed by the insensitivity of the nurse. Seeing Mama afraid upset me terribly. I just wanted to scoop her up somehow and get us out of there. We'd go someplace. We'd manage. It would all be okay. Oh god, I thought, I can't even get her out of bed myself, much less take her somewhere. We were both trapped in this frightening story.

Then it was time to wait again, something I could do more easily once Mama was in bed and reasonably comfortable. But it was Mama who did not find it so easy to rest. The paralysis had caused her left arm to contract in such a way that it lay, elbow bent, curled across her chest with her fingers closed into a fist. Indicating this poor arm, Mama said, "Honey, this thing is getting awfully heavy lying on me. Put it somewhere, will you?"

"I can't, Mama. That's your arm."

"Oh, come on. Just put it somewhere. I don't want it here. Put it in the closet."

"Mama," I pleaded, "I'm sorry." At the risk of appearing unwilling to help, I explained, "I wish I could put it somewhere for you, but I can't. It's attached to you. It's your left arm. Look at it. See? It's your arm." She didn't look.

She also expressed concern several times about her belongings, in response to which I would tell her that I had unpacked her things and put them into the dresser and closet. I would get up and show her what I meant. She was particularly concerned about her shoes, which now strikes me as poignant since she never again wore shoes.

That first day in the nursing home felt both interminable and dizzyingly swift. For the most part, Mama and I were left alone. Meals didn't amount to much. The staff had actually forgotten her at lunch time, so I had to ask for the meal. It took nearly two hours before a nurse came in, and then she spent barely a minute pouring the contents of a can into Mama's G-tube. Dinner was late, too. "We've had three other 'admits' today," one of the staff told me. I could only hope that by tomorrow Mama's presence would be integrated into their routine.

I stayed as late as I could. The sun had set, but I didn't turn on the light. The darkness was soothing as I sat there next to Mama's bed, watching her doze. The hour finally came when I knew I had to go. Mama seemed to be resting well. I thought she might be asleep, but I wasn't sure, so I began to speak softly to her, just in case she was listening. Off and on all day I had been explaining things to her, things that I thought would reassure and comfort her, things that at least *ought* to be true. I told her again that she would be safe in this place, that they would take care of her, that Aunt Margaret would come to see her every day, that she would have a phone installed soon, and that I would call her.

I refrained from telling Mama that I was going back to Santa Fe, as I would continue to refrain from doing each visit. That kind of information didn't matter anymore. In times to come, I would simply tell her I had to go, but I would be back. I didn't want her to feel like it was a big going away. I don't know if she could tell the difference among a lengthy absence, an overnight absence, or my stepping out for a bite to eat. She always took the news impassively that I was leaving and was always glad to see me when I returned, despite how brief or how long my absence. Mainly on that first night, though, I told her how very, very much I loved her, longing to leave her as full of that as I could. Suddenly, Mama's voice came out of the dark, strong and clear. "I love you, too, sweetheart, very much. Try to stay alive and take care of yourself."

It felt like she had reached across an abyss and touched a nerve, struck a chord deep in my being. If this story were a movie, the camera would cut to my sorrowful face. You would see me stand up falteringly, and then slowly walk out of the darkened room into the glaring light of the hallway. My face would be distorted by choked back tears. You would see me walk down the corridor as though I were walking the plank, shoulders held stiffly, looking straight ahead.

I glanced sideways at an aide who had been in the room earlier, hoping she would look back with knowing sympathy. She didn't. She just stared, blankly and coldly. She was a big woman with bleached-blonde hair, cropped short. Her lips were thin, or maybe it was that they were so pursed. And those eyes. So empty. So ungiving.

Leaving Mama in that nursing home was the most miserable thing I have ever done. I felt so helpless, so sad. I didn't want this for her. I didn't want it for me. I felt as though I were abandoning her. I have felt bad ever since for not having arranged for a longer visit while Mama was getting used to the nursing home, even though I knew Aunt Margaret would be there the next day to see her. I also knew that Mama was exhausted from the whole ordeal—enduring the stroke, being in the hospital, undergoing the surgery, and now moving to yet another unwelcoming place. I appreciated that she needed to rest. And so did I. I was literally ready to drop from fatigue. I had reached that point where people have to refuel or they are of no use at all. I decided that maybe it was best that I leave now, and that thought got me to the car. I sat there in the dark parking lot and sobbed.

Finally, reluctantly but resolutely, I pulled away from the nursing home and headed across town. My flight back to New Mexico was very early the next morning, so I had made arrangements to spend the night at a motel across from the airport. I had planned my route from the nursing home to the airport with the help of the map at Sandy's house. It was a simple route: turn left out of the nursing home, left again at the next light, and go straight until coming to I-465, the freeway that surrounds the city. Get on that heading west until coming to the airport exit, then take two right turns to the motel. Great. Easy. Except that the freeway entrance was closed for construction, and I had no idea where the next entrance was.

Since I-465 is circular, there is no way simply to drive parallel to it until coming to another ramp. Nearby businesses were closed for the night, so I couldn't ask anyone for directions. I was going to have to figure out an alternate route on my own. I remembered noticing on the map that Morris Street went through town to the airport and to the motel where I had reserved a room. Morris Street had caught my eye and lodged in my memory because this had also been the route to my grandmother's house.

Since the death of my grandmother, "Mom," in 1974, I had never been back to her neighborhood, had never wanted to go near there again. Over the years I had heard snatches of conversations—something about Eli Lilly & Company buying up the neighborhood for a planned expansion of its facilities, how property values had plummeted, and how eventually the house had been torn down. But I never really listened. In my mind it was preserved perfectly, just as it was the last time I had seen Mom in it, and it did not exist in time beyond that. I couldn't bear the thought of Mom's house without her, let alone the world without Mom or the world without her house. She had lived there my whole life, and my mother's whole life, too. It was more than a house; it was a family icon. It was sacred.

With more than a little trepidation, I headed north through the dark city and then west along Morris Street. Everything began to take on an ephemeral quality, generated probably by the dark, my exhaustion, and the present feeling of unfamiliarity imposed over some deep, old familiarity. Within moments, the sign for Kentucky Street loomed before me, and I knew I was entering Mom's neighborhood. Should I just zoom past the street, or should I veer left and take the few blocks through the core of the neighborhood before reconnecting with Morris Street? I guess I'm not one to buck fate. There I was, after all. I veered. Nordyke Street. I recited my grandmother's address and then her phone number, the old-fashioned way, using a word to represent the first two digits of the telephone number. My memory brought images of faces and activity and thriving life. But in reality only a few houses were left standing on the dark, deserted street. They stood ghostlike, surrounded by vacant lots, like the aftermath of some catastrophe.

It was as though a piece of my life had been erased, a whole piece of my family's history gone, with nothing to show that we had ever been there. The little brick school I had attended just across the alley was still standing, but with crude boards nailed over broken windows. It looked so abandoned and lonely. My mother had gone to that school some forty years before I did, and now all the life was gone from it. I slowly drove on, thinking about how something can be there and then not be there, and how a family's connectedness can persist despite all that seems lost.

I have often joked that going to Indianapolis is like returning to the scene of the crime. On this particular trip, commuting from Sandy's house on the north side to the hospital on the south side had, in effect, taken me through all the chapters of my life in that city, except for the times I had spent in my grandmother's neighborhood. Now, thanks to a closed freeway entrance, I revisited that, too. I found I had not only passed through the old neighborhoods, but I had also passed through the memories of my life. I discovered some very important things. Along with the hurts and disappointments that had helped propel my eventual exodus from Indianapolis to points west, there had also been a lot of fun and learning and love that rounded out the picture.

After a while, as memory after memory played itself out on the screen of my mind, it occurred to me that my life was ultimately okay, that it had just been the

way it was. Like many people, I had always found much
to find fault with in my early years, but, suddenly, for the
first time in my life, I realized I no longer needed my
childhood or my youth to have been any different from
what it was. Under the circumstances, this insight came
as a bittersweet freedom, one that has brought much
peace to my life and has been a silver lining in the cloud
of Mama's ordeal.

I went back to Santa Fe in the morning, worked
for a couple of days, then went to a friend's house in the
country, where I didn't even attempt to get out of bed for
two full days. I didn't pick up a book or turn on the TV.
I'm not sure I even had any thoughts. I just lay there,
mostly asleep, or awake and simply waiting again, waiting to feel revived enough to live some more of my life.
A riot of disruptions and losses had occurred on several
fronts within just a few months. I knew that I was going
to have to learn to pace myself in order to deal with it all,
and, most important, to be there effectively for Mama.

6

No Glory

White hairs are a crown of honor.
Proverbs 16:31

If a family has one old person in it, it possesses
a jewel.
Chinese Proverb

WHEN I WAS TEN or so I lived for a time with
my grandmother in her big wooden frame house on
Nordyke Street. This house was as worn and comfortable as the proverbial old shoe, steeped in the history of
four generations of my family and dating back more
than a century. Next door was the only brick house in
the neighborhood. It had a fortress-like presence, con-
firming its distinction from the other houses. It was
occupied by a middle-aged widow and her widowed
mother, and it provided shelter for them as well as for
several mysterious people, older and frailer than any I
had ever seen before. In contrast, my grandmother was
in her early seventies by then, and she was quite vigorous and independent.

The place seemed shrouded in secrecy, as did its
white-haired, ancient inhabitants, most of whom were

never seen save for an occasional motionless body sitting in a chair on the porch. White hair and pale skin seemed to merge with the light-colored, nondescript garments and covers in which the people were usually wrapped. I felt drawn to the old ones and longed to go near them, but I was always admonished to keep away, as though the mere presence of a child would do some great harm.

Years later, in my late teens, I was waiting at a bus stop in a different neighborhood. I struck up a conversation with a bright, genteel, elderly woman, who disclosed that she was a resident of a nearby nursing home. Cheerfully, I remarked that it must be pleasant to have her needs looked after and to live among others her age. "It's not home, honey," she replied, and her eyes pierced mine. Her words reverberated in my mind for years.

When I was twenty-three years old, I was looking for a job and met a nurse who urged me to apply at the nursing home where she worked. I soon found myself employed as a nurse aide, despite having no experience or background in such work. My memories of that place are images of ancient humans, withered and distorted, many slack-jawed and drooling, staring at me silently. I remember being told to change one elderly woman's bedding, only to find that her body was so stiff that I could not turn her. When someone finally came to help me, I was horrified to see big open wounds on her backside—my first sight of bed sores.

I have always been fond of old people, so perhaps it is not surprising that they kept weaving their way into my life. In my mid-twenties I was lured by an employment ad that promoted an alternative to nursing homes.

My boss, an enterprising woman, had turned the house next door to hers into what we would now call an assisted-living residence for senior citizens. The house provided a homey atmosphere, very much in contrast to typical hospital-like nursing homes. Six to eight people could live there at any given time, one or two residents to a bedroom.

One tall, craggy old man who resided there had been given a lobotomy, supposedly to eradicate his history of violent outbursts. He was certainly compliant now; he had apparently lost the ability to speak and seldom showed any interest in anything. Once when I was helping him to eat, he poked his finger into a small hole in the knee of my corduroys and grinned mischievously. I grinned back and teased him about it. A scolding from the owner, however, quickly sent him back into his torpor, and she scolded me, too, for "encouraging" him.

Two of the women who were roommates there didn't seem to have anything physically wrong with them but were probably suffering from Alzheimer's disease, though this label was not common then. During the day, the women tended to be quiet and submissive, except for the one who often escaped and had to be retrieved from around the neighborhood, a situation that vexed the owner considerably. Fortunately, the neighbors grew familiar with the situation and walked the woman home whenever they saw her out and about.

These two ladies grew very dear to me, especially when I once worked a night shift. That morning around three o'clock, I noticed a light shining out from their door, which was slightly ajar. I went to investigate and found that they had pulled all their clothes from the closet and spread them out on their beds. They proceeded to try on each other's outfits and parade in front of the full-length mirror in their room. I watched unnoticed from the hallway. I knew I was supposed to go in and make them go back to bed, but they were having such a good time that I decided to leave them alone and let them enjoy their fashion show. When the owner learned of the episode, she was not amused. She banished me from the night shift, lest I allow the ladies additional nocturnal activities.

At one point another woman, who had recently had a colostomy, joined the household. She was a well-groomed, meticulous lady and suffered grievously at having to wear a plastic bag attached to her abdomen to collect her feces. Her depression was largely ignored; the message she was getting was to buck up. Her mental condition deteriorated rapidly.

Although the owner was effusively affectionate toward her charges whenever outsiders visited, the rest of the time she was cool and stern, brooking very little aggravation from the people in her care. In addition to ordering them about and threatening them with such punishment as loss of privileges (much like some people treat children), she made liberal use of psychotropic medications to control behavior. Those who complained were soon shuffling about with vacant eyes and nothing to say.

A few years later I was anticipating the start of graduate school. I needed a job with flexible hours to accommodate my class schedule as well as one that would supplement the new holistic health business I had launched. Eager for an opportunity to put my holistic health skills to work, I answered an appealing ad from a company seeking people to provide health care for the elderly.

I became a floating nurse aide for a registry that provided health care aides to people's homes as well as supplemental staff to nursing homes. Many nursing homes, perennially short of staff, use such agencies widely. Although this sort of service sounds helpful, I found that it actually contributes to problems in the current nursing home system: residents frequently end up being cared for by nurses and aides who do not know them and who are not familiar with their needs and routines. The nursing homes I worked in varied somewhat in cleanliness, chaos, and organization as well as in the quality and timeliness of the care provided. Some of the staff were conscientious about providing me with the particulars of an individual's care; others were too busy and overwhelmed to bother.

The work was quite challenging, with lots of bending, reaching, and lifting. Although I had a slight frame and weighed barely one hundred pounds, I hoisted people more than half again my size in and out of beds and chairs, with or without someone to assist me. Back injuries are endemic among nurse aides, but my holistic health training had included back care, so I was able to implement ways of moving and lifting that protected me.

Sometimes, though, someone got away from me. I had gotten one very round lady out of her chair but found I could neither manage the few inches to the bed nor the distance back to the chair. The main thing in my mind at that moment was to protect her and her no-doubt-brittle bones; there was no way I was going to let her drop. For a second, we were suspended. "We're going down," I told her. "It's okay, though—I've got you." And then we sank, as if in slow motion and as gracefully as in a ballet. I cushioned her against my thighs until we were both sitting on the floor. Carefully squirming out from under her, I guided her arm to clutch the bed rail for support, and I ran for help.

Working in a nursing home means being busy constantly, always being assigned more residents than one can optimally care for in the time allotted. I was typically given a long roster of people to attend to, many of whom could not walk and some of whom could not move on their own. On day shifts, all the residents had to be gotten out of bed, bathed, dressed, and groomed. Those who could not feed themselves had to be fed. The beds had to be changed and the laundry disposed of. I often felt conflicted knowing that I had to complete this basic care for everyone on my roster but wanting to respect both the dignity and the hygiene needs of those who were incontinent by promptly cleaning and changing them. On the top of this, it was very frustrating to find that a resident had soiled herself just when you thought she was all set. The task of keeping residents clean and dry was compounded sometimes to the point of impossibility when clean linens and diapers ran out, a not uncommon occurrence in many nursing homes.

It was demoralizing to leave at the end of a shift knowing I had not performed all the tasks I should have.

Cutting corners was the only way to get the basic necessities covered for each of the residents assigned to me. Skipping oral hygiene and nail care and not changing marginally dirty clothes and linens were the least of the ways that allowed the aides to get by. At the same time, families are rightfully upset when these tasks are not performed promptly and as often as needed. There is one, and only one, solution, which is to have enough aides on duty at all times so that no resident has to wait too long a time before receiving the appropriate care.

So many of the elders I cared for were fragile and uncertain, requiring a tenderness and patience that was at odds with the brisk pace of completing their care on time. This was certainly the case when it came to giving baths. I had learned from taking care of children how distressing baths could be if the water was too hot or if the washings were too vigorous—and how much more difficult the children would then make the job for me. Elders who usually balked at bath time became models of cooperation when I took a moment to let them test the water before they submitted themselves to it. I washed them gently and tried to honor any requests they made about how to proceed. This approach increased my efficiency, eliminating the time and energy wasted struggling with the bathers. Apparently, the aides around me had never been taught this straightforward method, because I often heard them complaining about the difficult times they had bathing residents with whom I had had no trouble at all.

The pressure to hurry, however, can effectively counteract any desire aides may have to perform their duties gently and thoroughly. Equally sad is that aides often are forced to skip the few moments they might have taken to chat with residents, to make the residents feel they are still people who matter and not just tasks to be completed. Socializing and making contact with the elders can become an unaffordable luxury, yet even back then, I knew how important it was and snatched whatever moments with them I could. Many people dismiss their conversations with the elderly as being superficial, unimportant, and boring. I have learned that conversing about the weather is more worthwhile than I ever would have thought possible, because it is not so much the content of the interaction that makes a difference for these elders—it is the contact.

If you talk long enough with most elders, you will surely get around to one topic that is never far from their minds: death. Despite its frequency and inevitability within the nursing home environment, death was a subject vigorously avoided by the staff in the nursing homes I worked. When elderly residents did make some reference to death, particularly the notion that their own demise was imminent, they were often chided or cajoled. "You die? Why, you'll probably outlive us all." "You're fine. Just eat your lunch and you'll feel better." Although the work pioneered by Elisabeth Kübler-Ross and the hospice movement has made important inroads into our culture's disconnect on this subject, the death process is still surrounded by considerable denial and avoidance in many medical settings.

It is a paradox of nursing homes that, on the one hand, their nature forces residents closer and closer to social and psychological withdrawal, but on the other hand, caregivers try to prevent residents from relinquishing their grip on the world and from turning inward to complete their end-of-life process. I have often seen well-meaning caregivers, whether family members or staff, badgering elderly people to eat and be dressed and bathed when the elder is just begging to be allowed to let go. Similarly, there are those who beg to forego the medications that they know are prolonging their lives. Sadly, the distinction is seldom made between someone who is depressed and needs that condition addressed, and someone who is preparing to die.

In one facility I heard some aides and nurses speaking with annoyance about a woman who was "going on" about dying. I visited this woman several times during the following days. The first time I went in, she rolled her eyes and said, "I'm dying," in a hollow way that bespoke the number of times she had repeated the phrase to deaf ears.

"Are you?" I replied matter-of-factly.

She started a bit, opening her eyes wide and looking at me. I stroked her head and she relaxed a little. "Yes, I think so," she said softly, sounding very genuine.

"Do you think it will be soon?"

"I don't know," she said, her voice trailing off.

"Well, it's okay, you know. It's okay to die. You can go whenever the time comes."

"I can?"

"Sure," I told her. After that we talked several times, often in the dark after she had been put to bed for the night. Her daughter, whose visit she had been anxiously awaiting, came to see her. She seemed relieved. Then, during the night a week or so later, she slipped into death's embrace.

Unfortunately, many residents in nursing homes are no longer able to verbalize their feelings. One woman, who had been a physician, was in her early nineties and required round-the-clock care after having lost both speech and mobility. Every day the nurse brought this woman her medication. But the former doctor knew too well that the pills she was being given were forcing her tired heart to keep beating, and so she would clamp her jaws shut tight and glare at the perpetuator of her suffering. And every day the nurse would force the woman's ancient jaws open, stuff the pills inside, close the jaws, and then repeat the intrusion to be sure the pills had been swallowed.

Working in many nursing home settings has had a profound effect on how I view aging and eldercare in this culture. I see nursing home staff problems as a product of both a society that has made care of the aged a low priority and a system that has been more oriented to exploitation than to service. The organization of a typical nursing home does not encourage nurses and aides to be as compassionate as they can be and to provide the highest quality and most sensitive care for their charges. Quite the contrary, they are put in a position where consistent quality care is all but impossible.

I have seen firsthand that nurses and aides are under considerable pressure to accomplish more tasks than they are reasonably allotted time for and are often without the necessary supplies to perform their duties effectively and appropriately. This is clearly a reflection of a system that is weighted more heavily toward financial productivity than it is toward sensitive quality care of elderly and disabled people. Despite regulations for resident-aide ratios, aides routinely have too many residents to provide adequate care for, and the residents suffer from the ensuing neglect.

The frustrating situation is little better for LPNs and RNs. They are responsible for dispensing medicines and providing treatments; overseeing aides; handling complaints and concerns from family members and residents; as well as completing a burdensome amount of paperwork. The ratio of all nurses to residents is often so low that the nurses seldom have the opportunity to spend more than a few minutes with any one resident. Investors, on the other hand, benefit from having the least number of aides and nurses on duty at any given time. The accountants who measure the efficiency of nursing homes do not count such things as the number of times the staff evokes a smile from a resident.

Lack of adequate training further contributes to the substandard care in nursing homes. Despite the fact that nurse aides must now be certified, there are some areas in which they are still woefully undertrained. I have observed many aides who not only lack the necessary skills for the physical care of elderly people but also seem completely oblivious to the elders' psychological and social needs. As a result, countless incidents of dehumanizing insensitivity occur in nursing homes every day.

I have often seen aides become offended and resentful when an elder lashes out at them. Taking it as a personal affront, the aides seem to think the elder purposefully wants to interfere with their efforts. They seem unable to imagine how the elder might be experiencing the situation, and their response is to become defensive, hostile, cold, indifferent, or patronizing to their charges.

Nursing home administrators, supervisors, owners, and government regulators have to stop tolerating insensitive and inept behavior on the part of the caretaking staff. Giving nurse aides more extensive instruction in understanding and responding to the psychological, emotional, and social needs of the residents would go a long way toward transforming how they interact with residents. This new knowledge and behavior could radically transform the entire nursing home environment.

Some people working in nursing homes are just not cut out for it. No amount of training will supply them with the necessary aplomb, good humor, and understanding to do the job well. They, along with the dangerous minority who are intentionally malicious, need to be identified. Currently there is no federal regulation requiring criminal background checks for prospective nursing home employees. As a result, twenty-five percent of the people who have been prosecuted for abuse in nursing homes and five percent of all nursing home employees have been found to have criminal records (as reported by the American Health Care Association). Clearly, people who cannot be entrusted with the care of defenseless elderly citizens should be weeded out.

Critics of nursing homes reason that cultural disdain for nursing home work along with the low pay and high demands of the job eliminate many who would be capable of providing the kind of care that should be routine in all nursing homes. They claim that the low pay also leads to employees who are the least educated and least experienced members of society, thereby making good care the exception, not the rule. While I cannot deny that there may be truth to this, it does not in itself explain poor care. I have seen dedicated, hard-working aides with limited educational and economic backgrounds who are impeded far more by the circumstances of their employment than by their backgrounds. If it weren't for all the courageous and devoted souls who are drawn to nursing homes out of the goodness of their hearts, the horrors would likely be compounded beyond belief.

Many nurse aides prefer their jobs to other jobs that would be much less meaningful. Some of the best aides have told me they care for the residents in the way they hope their own parent will be cared for should the time come. They are the real gems who dispense love with every gesture, in stark contrast to those who become as hardened and callous as you might expect a prison guard to be.

I cannot emphasize enough how demanding—physically, mentally, and emotionally—the work of a nurse aide is. Even those who start out very caring often survive by walling themselves off from feelings, whether their own or those of the people they are ministering to. Many times I have seen aides do their work mechanically, going through the motions, sometimes efficiently, sometimes not, but just not quite *there*. I felt that way myself at times as a nurse aide but fought against it. I couldn't allow myself to depersonalize the people I was taking care of.

The way most nursing homes are run guarantees deteriorating morale among employees. Burnout from overwork is common. And a less discussed but not infrequent source of burnout is being aware of the mistreatment of elders while feeling powerless to do anything about it. The societal factor—that nursing home personnel are some of the most underpaid people in the work force doing a bottom-end job—undermines commitment to the work. These things must change before the elderly and disabled can hope for a level of care that reflects the dignity and compassion that is due them.

Although efforts are being made to keep staff on the job, including a slight rise in wages for nursing home workers in recent years, turnover rates continue to be high. On average a nurse aide lasts only two years, with many nurses not far behind. Interestingly, those who care and are trying hard to do a good job, and those who need the job but resent the kind of work they must do, seem to burn out equally fast. I became increasingly worn down from working as a nurse aide. It was seldom the residents who made the job feel so difficult, it was the unrelenting rigor of the pace, the physical demands, and the discouraging feeling of always being behind.

Since the first time I ever saw a nursing home from the inside, I fervently did not want my mother to end up in one. Over the years I regaled Mama with grim stories of what the inhabitants of such facilities endured, hoping that she would be inspired to take better care of herself. I believed that it was in her power to avoid such a fate. As she aged and began to incur increasing infirmities, I spent many years trying to direct her life in some way, exhorting her to exercise, to improve her diet, to take vitamins. I mentioned anything that I thought might help stave off disease and disability. I wanted so much to protect her, but how do you protect someone from old age and death?

During the long months Mama lived in the nursing home, I often reflected on the irony of being "on the other side of the bed." Working as a nurse aide had prepared me for the schedule and ministrations my mother would be subjected to, as well as for the great time and effort that would be involved in her care. I had been sensitized to the dilemma of providing care to dependent elders. Nothing, however, could have prepared me for how it would feel to have my mother be the helpless old lady lying in the bed, knowing she could not tell anyone what happened or even understand everything that was happening to her.

The compassion I felt for the residents when I was an aide didn't come close to the gut-wrenching agony I often felt about my mother's plight. I also had no idea how uninformed and powerless a family member could feel. I had been anything but sensitive to what the families may have been going through. With youthful self-righteousness and inexperience, I believed that these families had abandoned their elders, and I judged them accordingly, so sure that I would never let *my* mother end up in such circumstances. I behaved more kindly toward family members who seemed solicitous and visited regularly, and I felt disdain for those who came infrequently, left quickly, and tried to ignore the whole situation. Little did I know that I was undergoing training that would someday enable me not to follow suit and flee in frustration and bewilderment.

7

TOTAL CARE

What do you see, nurses? What do you see?
What are you thinking when you're looking at me?
A crabbit old woman, not very wise,
Uncertain of habit with faraway eyes . . .
Who dribbles her food and makes no reply
When you say in a loud voice, "I do wish you'd try."
Who seems not to notice the things that you do,
And forever is losing a stocking or shoe.
Who, unresisting or not, lets you do as you will,
When bathing and feeding, the long day to fill.
Is that what you are thinking, is that what you see?
Then open your eyes, nurse, you are not looking at ME.
part of a poem found in the belongings of a geriatric
patient in Scotland after her death

WITHIN A FEW MONTHS of Mama's stroke, it
became evident that she might be in for a long haul at
the nursing home. Her doctor advised us that although
she could die suddenly for any number of reasons, she
could just as well persist as she was for many years.
Knowing this, I planned to come back to see her at regular intervals, but I was constrained by financial consid-
erations. I was self-employed, which meant a loss of

income for every day that I missed work. I decided to juggle my schedule so that I could come for long weekends, which reduced the financial loss. I could afford to visit Mama more often by making these long weekend visits than by coming for extended periods of time. I also wanted to be at the nursing home on both weekdays and weekends to observe Mama's care at different times and to be on hand when administrators, supervisors, and doctors were available for consultation. I tried to visit every three months, although circumstances sometimes made me come sooner or delay a little longer. Still, the whole situation never felt quite balanced. I was always exhausted by the time I left, and I felt like I never stayed long enough or came often enough. I was never confident about leaving Mama alone in the nursing home, yet her care often wasn't any better when I was right there next to her.

My commitment to see my mother through her stay in the nursing home, to advocate for her, and to protect her as best I could was unwavering. At the same time, I saw the necessity of accepting my limitations. I knew that I could not possibly address everything that bothered me, that I was not going to be able to make that place into my vision of a nursing home, where *all* the elders—including Mama—received the kind of care they ought to. So I established a rhythm by facing the problems as they came up, dealing with each one, one at a time, and then moving on. I tried not to get discouraged as some of the same issues repeatedly presented themselves. In fact, I knew that in the long run my persistence might have little impact on the way things were

done there. I could only do the best job I could by looking out for my mother and by being with her during this
time in her life.

One day I was discussing some issues with a nurse,
and she referred to my mother as a "total care." This
term really stopped me in my tracks. I realized what it
meant, but what I wanted it to mean was something very
different. I wanted it to mean that Mama would, in this
twilight of her long, arduous life, have the comfort of
being totally cared for by someone else, with all her
needs met and her well-being assured. I wanted it to
mean that the suffering inherent to her condition would
be mitigated as much as possible. But what it really
meant, most of the time, was far removed from my idyl-
lic picture.

"Total care" residents can no longer perform any of
the functions of daily living and therefore must have
everything done for them. They are the most strenuous
and time-consuming residents to take care of. They are
the ones who most frustrate and tire overworked nurse
aides. They are also the ones who are the most vulnerable. Many are not able to let others know if they need
something, and their cries and moans often go unheed-
ed. They also are more likely to lack the ability to protest
when they disagree with some aspect of their care.
Consequently, they more readily become victims of
neglect and mistreatment.

In many facilities, total care residents are housed in
the back wards or upper floors, segregated from more
highly functioning individuals. Some elders in total care
wards are physically well but suffer from pronounced

disorientation. They tend to be stigmatized and misunderstood, and consequently they are denied opportunities to participate in stimulating activities they are still capable of. Other elders are psychologically oriented but are significantly incapacitated physically. They are the ones who must endure being trapped in bodies that prevent them from participating in those activities they are still capable of mentally. And finally, there are the elders, like my mother, who have been ravaged on all fronts, betrayed by both body and mind, and are therefore most cut off from the activities of daily living. Although total care residents encompass a wide range of conditions and capacities, these elders all are lumped together, for years on end, with little accommodation to their individual needs and abilities.

Being a total care resident in a typical nursing home means losing control over virtually all aspects of one's daily life. Not only does it mean being awakened in the morning according to the facility's agenda, it also means being awakened or intruded on at any time during the day or night so that various aides and nurses can do their jobs. When a person eats, is bathed, takes medicine, goes to bed, or sits in a chair, the activity takes place according to the convenience and scheduling needs of the facility, and seldom as a response to the needs or desires of the resident.

Indeed, routine can create a sense of security, and it can contribute to orientation. These benefits, however, are undermined by schedules that frustrate and distress those who must abide by them. A common scene in nursing homes occurs every evening after supper when exhausted total care residents are left sitting in their various conveyances, sometimes for more than two hours before an aide comes to put them to bed. Some of them cry out, begging for someone to assist them. The luckier ones are able to doze while they wait. Imagine tonight when you are tired and ready for bed, having to sit up for another two hours in a chair that you've already been sitting in for hours, waiting for someone to put you to bed. Then imagine having to wait like that every night for the rest of your life.

Social and psychological needs are no less important than physical needs, but they are the needs more easily, and therefore more likely to be, ignored. Aides and nurses might greet the person they are caring for, but they often do not take the time to explain what they are about to do, much less listen to what the resident might have to say about how it is done. The aide who takes things slowly and takes time to socialize with an elder who is about to have her body handled in a highly intimate manner can make a huge difference. The potentially dehumanizing experience becomes a considerate, cooperative effort.

Being familiar with their caregivers can enable all nursing home residents to feel more comfortable and more secure in knowing what to expect. Instead, due to staff turnover and rotation policies, what often happens is that dependent elders endure a constantly changing cast of caretakers. These staff people frequently enter residents' rooms, unannounced, and proceed to bathe them, change them, dress and undress them—without so much as an introduction.

One of the most intrusive events in the lives of total care residents who typically can no longer feed themselves, is being fed by people whom they may not even know, who proceed to shovel food into their mouths, often with little regard for whether they are hungry or like the food. It is not uncommon to see apathetic aides feeding elders in a mechanical manner, without looking at or otherwise connecting with the persons they are feeding, while conversing among themselves over the heads of the unfortunate recipients of this behavior.

To add further to these demoralizing circumstances, staff as well as family members tend to speak *about* disoriented residents in the residents' presence, referring to them in the third person. The speakers are oblivious to the fact that even highly disoriented people are often still capable of experiencing embarrassment, humiliation, and other kinds of emotional pain. Attitudes and behaviors that deny awareness, rather than allow for the possibility of awareness, seem to prevail.

Many total care residents are still capable of making choices regarding the events of their daily lives, but they are seldom given the opportunity to do so. Something as simple for an aide as holding up two blouses and asking, "Which one would you like to wear today, Mrs. Smith?" is all too rare. Thoughtfulness is undermined by professionals and family members who readily argue that many of these elders are no longer aware of what is happening and that efforts to make contact with them are pointless. As a result, many dependent elderly people soon find a way to distance themselves even further in order to cope with the alienating treatment they receive.

More than fifty percent of the residents of nursing homes are considered to be suffering from some type of dementia. Most of these residents are housed in the total care wards where their mental health needs are virtually ignored. Evidence suggests that many residents of nursing homes become disoriented in a fairly short period of time following their admittance, and those who come in already disoriented tend to get increasingly more so. Elders who are systematically stripped of any sense of autonomy, who are chastised for any behavior but submission, and who have little hope of their lives getting any better, gradually unravel in the face of such circumstances. As the months pass, with lack of stimulation exacerbating the situation, the disorientation builds, and many of the residents who did not start out in the total care section of a nursing home end up there. And once there, they seldom regain the level of functioning necessary to leave. Instead of offering the atmosphere of a home or a community that might enable residents to flourish for a time, nursing homes slowly erase individual lives through the blandness and regimentation of institutionalization.

Regulations require that the elderly be given a mental health evaluation before being admitted to a nursing home. This regulation was put into effect so that elders whose primary diagnosis is psychiatric will be sent to mental health facilities for assistance rather than to nursing homes. However, this requirement is automatically waived when an elder is diagnosed with cognitive impairment. Thus, elders who do have a mental illness may be sent to nursing homes anyway. As the pre-existing psychological problems continue and new ones develop, many disoriented elderly people display disruptive behaviors such as crying out or being physically or verbally abusive. The common response in many nursing homes to these circumstances is to administer some form of chemical restraint—drugs. While genuine forms of mental illness (the most common of which is depression) should not be left untreated, a psychological evaluation should be done before a resident is given a prescription for a psychotropic medication. The drug should be intended as a treatment and not as a behavioral control. This is a kind of drug abuse, and it is just as inappropriate and inhumane as any other.

Moreover, when uncooperative or combative behavior leads total care residents to be labeled belligerent, their symptoms need to be addressed rather than suppressed. Too often what happens is that the staff or the facility lets its own needs take precedence over the elders' situations. A vicious cycle develops: (1) An elder becomes agitated by conditions in the nursing home, such as constant and distressing background noise, shortcomings in care, and overwhelming boredom. (2) No effort is made to alleviate the conditions. (3) The elders' aggressive reactions escalate. (4) More stringent, suppressive measures are put in place by the nursing home staff. And on and on it goes.

Thus, it is a mistake to assume that mental illness is simply more prevalent among elders than it is in the rest of the population. Numerous psychological studies

have indicated that anyone can quickly manifest symptoms of mental illness if put under distressing enough
circumstances—especially when they feel helpless to
alter those circumstances. Recent studies have also found
a significant connection between distressing life events
and the onset of Alzheimer's type disorders. Many elders
and their families lack the skills to deal with traumatic
experiences and do not get the help they need at the
time. Further, it appears that some of the defense mechanisms that keep in check a person's emotions around
unresolved issues break down in extreme old age. Instead
of the typical medical approach of viewing this as a
pathological phenomenon and therefore trying to suppress the occurrences, elders would be better served if
they were supported in the process of resolving their life
issues.

It is particularly sad that among these most debilitated folks, whose bodies will soon fail no matter what
is done, their souls are utterly abandoned. At best, nursing homes go through the motions of addressing residents' mental health needs by using ineffective
methods, such as reality orientation, for which funding
is available. Meanwhile, less conventional methods that
have demonstrated outstanding success but are not medically reimbursable are financially out of reach for the
residents who could most benefit from them. It remains
to be discovered to what extent elders' faculties might be
restored or to what extent their deterioration might be
slowed if their psycho-emotional difficulties were effectively treated.

Although the psychological difficulties that unfold

in nursing homes are undoubtedly the result of a lifetime's accumulation of unresolved issues, this does not
adequately account for the mental deterioration that so
frequently occurs after admission to these institutions. It
is more likely that the coping mechanisms that elders
develop against the often hideous and generally hopeless
nature of their situations are mistaken for various forms
of mental illness. In some nursing homes the atmosphere of despair is palpable.

Some elderly people cope simply by refusing to
accept the fact that they are living in a nursing home at
all. Instead, they insist that they are just visiting, that it
is a temporary stay, and that so-and-so will be coming to
take them home this afternoon, tomorrow, or next week.
The weeks stretch into months and then into years, but
the elders don't give up. It is not unusual for some of
them to beg family members, or anyone else whose
attention they can catch, to take them home. Maybe
believing that it is a mistake or something temporary is
what enables them to deal with the dreary, relentless
sameness of one day after another. Maybe their denial
keeps at bay the knowledge that this is what their life has
come to, that nothing lies ahead but deterioration and
death.

In tribute to the endurance of the human spirit,
even the most feeble of total care residents will sometimes rail against their fate. Relieved of lifelong social
constraints, many of them express their feelings power-
fully and directly, clearly releasing pressure by venting
against those around them. It is not uncommon, nor
unreasonable under the circumstances, for those in the

back wards to at times lash out, cry out, resist against what is being done to them, and generally carry on, sometimes with words and sometimes with unmistakably provocative ululations.

Even the best-humored among the total care residents, which included my mother, can't keep up a cooperative demeanor all the time. When frustration overcame her, Mama would call the aides "little shits." They failed to see the humor in my mother, who had always been so ladylike, speaking to them in such language. Sometimes when I was there, she would include me in her tirade, to which I would respond, "Oh yeah? Well, you're an old poop, so I guess we're in good company." This always tickled Mama and lightened her mood, but it never succeeded in enlightening the aides, who persisted in their peevishness and acted as though they thought I was pretty strange for talking to my mother that way. Advising the aides outright that they should not take what Mama said personally was futile. It seems that invariably what prevails in response to these kinds of outbursts is to discourage the elders, treating them like recalcitrant children.

While nurses and nurse aides can leave their jobs at nursing homes whenever the atmosphere becomes too much to tolerate, the severely disabled residents of the back wards cannot leave and are essentially prisoners. Many of these elders do not have families or anyone else to advocate for them, and they cannot effectively, if at all, advocate for themselves.

Being moved to a different nursing home can sometimes provide relief for a particular problem, but this just as likely means trading one set of difficulties for another, and ultimately does nothing to solve the overall dilemma of being a dependent elderly person in the present nursing home system. For many, there are no better facilities available in their area. In addition, the "transfer trauma" of being moved to a new residence can be extremely hard on a fragile, old person. It appears that the ability to adapt to new circumstances diminishes with age, and that rapid deterioration and death are often the result of an elderly person being forced into unfamiliar surroundings. This is especially true for elders suffering from even a mild degree of confusion. For many individuals and families, it is the devil they have come to know that will always seem like the better bet.

Although all nursing home beds are outfitted with call buttons that ring at the nurses' station, many total care residents are incapable of using them. In addition, and despite regulations, the call buttons are not always within their reach. Even when residents do succeed in activating the buttons, the calls are frequently ignored and are considered a bother. Some residents use the buttons as a means of getting desired attention, but once they find themselves still alone, they give up. Some ring them anyway, again and again, maybe just because they can or maybe as a fruitless attempt to get some need met. It is a sad editorial on the desperation of many nursing home residents.

Other folks take to shouting out their needs, repeating themselves sometimes for hours until someone finally comes. Total care wards often wind up bearing a grim resemblance to psychiatric wards when the regular vocalizing in loud, strident tones becomes so repetitive that the litanies sound like bizarre, tortured chants. The voices become a part of the fabric of sound that is the constant background of the total care wards of many nursing homes. Being trapped in the vicinity of such behavior can be extremely distressing for some residents, while others may adapt, or maladapt, to it. In some way or another it takes a toll. One day, when you don't hear a familiar shouter, you sigh and know that that one has died.

For the majority of nursing home residents, having a roommate is inevitable. Although this arrangement is a potential means of preventing excessive isolation, the capacity for total care residents to become acquainted with their roommates, or any other residents, on their own is often quite limited. Poor eyesight and hearing thwart contact at any but the closest proximity. Limited mobility is a further impediment. Sometimes even the few feet separating two beds is an unbridgeable abyss. Adequate efforts are seldom made by the staff to facilitate familiarity between roommates. Consequently, residents may feel they are living in rooms with strangers. When total care residents are suspicious of their fellow inhabitants, perceiving them as potential threats, they tend to avoid each other as much as possible.

Not being offered socialization opportunities to become familiar with other residents, even one's own roommate, can naturally lead to mistrust. Sadly, family members sometimes feel compelled to participate in this dynamic, feeling they must protect their loved ones from those "others." People imagine that total care residents can't possibly provide or appreciate companionship. Those who look a little closer, however, may find these folks capable of more than they are given credit for. At the very least, even some of the most disabled residents might take comfort from another person's presence. Sometimes just knowing that someone else is close by can make a person feel less alone, but only if the circumstances are such that the other is perceived as harmless and perhaps even friendly.

In addition, a common indication of chaotic, inappropriate, and low-quality nursing home conditions is seen when trouble breaks out between residents. Too often the method of dealing with resident conflicts is simply to separate the offenders, to scold them, or to ignore the conflicts when all else fails. Social worker interventions, which generally occur only in response to a family complaint, are more likely to result in a logistical change than a therapeutic one. Occasionally, nursing home staff do come up with creative, problem-solving measures that further highlight how ineffective the usual responses are.

Mama's time in the nursing home soon exceeded the maximum number of weeks that Medicare would pay for, and she became not only a total care resident but also a Medicaid patient, which meant having to move her to what was referred to as a "Medicaid bed." It is a common practice in nursing homes to designate certain rooms and beds in this manner. It is a means for limiting the number of Medicaid patients accepted as well as for saving the better (larger) rooms for private-pay individuals, who usually pay the facility more per month than what it receives from those dependent on public funds.

When Mama was moved to the Medicaid ward, it was obvious that the rooms were smaller. But what I didn't realize until later was that the ratio of staff to residents was lower, and there were other reductions in service as well. Although it is against the law for nursing homes to discriminate against Medicaid patients, much of the literature on nursing homes reveals it is not an uncommon practice.

In essence, becoming a total care resident in a typical American nursing home means losing a great deal of personhood. It is as though the residents' physical needs become their identity, and the care they receive is directed solely at those physical needs. Many also suffer from feelings of isolation even when they are physically surrounded by many people. When I walk through the halls of a nursing home and see all the residents on view for anyone to look at, whether they are in their rooms or in common areas, I cannot help but feel that I am in a zoo. They may not be in cages, but they are no less confined and exposed, no less trapped and bored. This is what life becomes for millions of our elders. My sorrow that my mother had joined the ranks of these unfortunate citizens was constant.

8

MISSED OPPORTUNITIES AND MOMENTS SEIZED

True end is not in the reaching of the limit,
but in the completion which is limitless.
Rabindranath Tagore

MAMA SHARED HER new room for almost two years with a woman who also had sustained a stroke. Fortunately, the woman's family had opted for a unique arrangement of the furniture. Instead of their standard parallel placement, the beds were positioned at right angles to each other, which significantly increased the open space in the room. When we first met Mama's roommate, Doris, she seemed relatively well oriented but not able to say much, although when she did speak, her speech was clear. She could get around by wheelchair, so we didn't see much of her at first because she spent the whole day out of the room. She was a large woman with short, steely gray hair and a deep voice. I was startled one day when Mama referred to Doris as "he" and "that man." Mama apparently thought she had a male roommate and was taking it in stride.

As the months wore on, Doris's condition deteriorated. Her speech was increasingly filled with references
that no one else understood, and she was no longer able
to propel her wheelchair by herself. She also became
increasingly agitated. The aides started returning her to
the room after meals, leaving her to sit in her chair.
Doris would proceed to yell and bang things, calling to
the aides to come put her to bed. She often pressed her
call button, too, if it wasn't out of her reach. It was not
unusual for staff to take more than an hour to respond.
Once in bed, Doris would occasionally take a brief nap
but would soon awaken and begin yelling and banging
for someone to come get her up again. She also developed the habit of pulling the string that clicked on and
off the fluorescent light above her bed. Over and over
she would repeat the sequence—the banging and
yelling, the light blinking, the clicking sound of the
switch, the yelling and banging—until it became mad-
dening. I tried to talk with Doris. I tried to comfort and
soothe her. I even tried mildly reproaching her for making such a racket, but it was all to no avail. I had no idea
how to reach her, and no one else appeared to be trying.

I knew I had to act when one day while Mama
napped, I saw her twitch agitatedly whenever Doris
yelled. I felt some regret, as though we were abandoning
Doris, but to sit in that little room with her hollers and
general cacophony hour after hour was like being in
some kind of torture chamber. I had become used to
hearing such disturbances ricocheting through the halls,
but at least we could get some respite by closing the door
and shutting out the noise for a while. Without that

option, however, only a room change could provide relief. Unfortunately, this solution did nothing to assist Doris with her agitation, and we continued to hear her symphony of discord, mercifully muffled by the wall that separated us once Mama was relocated to an adjoining room.

Mama's next and final roommate, Helen, was in her nineties and was perennially in very low spirits, often weeping and speaking bitterly. She was given to lashing out at the nursing home staff and sometimes scolded them with such expressions as "dag gummit." Helen was also given to hurling rude epithets at Mama. Mama did not suffer this abuse kindly and did not hesitate to tell the offender to shut up. The nursing home staff made no attempt to help the roommates become more closely acquainted. Just having their chairs placed facing one another so they could get a good look at each other might have gone a long way toward helping them develop a sense of familiarity and comfort. I wish I had thought of it at the time.

A man occasionally visited Helen, but he always acted very anxious to be on his way. I overheard them once. Helen was begging him to take her home, and she was crying when he left. I went over and put my arms around her shoulders, trying to comfort her. She insisted she didn't belong in "this place," that she was there temporarily and was going to go home any day now.

When people lose the ability to express themselves, to find the words they need, they sometimes talk "in code." So when nursing home residents repeatedly tell relatives to take them home, that may be the only way they can express that they are feeling scared, lonely, or confused. Instead of responding to these underlying feelings, relatives may feel guilty and react defensively by pulling away, maybe even refusing to visit or visiting less frequently, in order to avoid these painful scenes.

It would not be unfair to call nursing homes a study in failed relationships. Not only do roommates get an unfair shake at becoming familiar with one another, but doctor/patient relationships are tenuous as well. All nursing home residents are required to have a personal physician who will oversee their overall treatment plans. In most communities only a few doctors are willing to make trips to nursing homes when their long-term patients are institutionalized, so many residents do not have the opportunity to continue with a physician who already knows them. Also, there can be a considerable difference in nursing home residents' care plans depending on the orientation of the doctor. Some doctors take a very passive, hands-off approach, while others pursue aggressive treatment strategies. There are doctors who will not hesitate to dialyze, intubate, or take a scalpel to even the oldest and sickest of patients. Ideally, families or residents should select doctors with geriatric training if any are available. These doctors are specifically trained in the health issues of elderly people and are more likely to withhold vigorous interventions that are designed to prolong life, taking time to consider the emotional or psychological suffering of the patient before prescribing a treatment.

Mama had three doctors during her nursing home stay, and they seemed to cover the spectrum. The first one, Dr. Short, came well recommended and had many other patients in the facility. He was an older man, continuing to practice when others might have retired. My first hint that he may not be the man for the job came when he displayed an utter disinterest in my mother's prior medical history. Satisfaction plummeted further when I would finally reach him on the telephone only to find that he did not actually know who my mother was. It seems he made rounds once a month and paid his patients an amicable visit of about five minutes for which he billed forty dollars. According to the aides, he rarely examined any of his patients during that time, and he complied with nurses' requests for treatment by simply signing orders.

While Mama's second physician initially seemed to be a great improvement because of his much increased involvement with her, Dr. Klink was not specifically trained in geriatrics and consequently did not always pursue a care plan appropriate to someone for whom death, not recovery, would be the eventual outcome. (For most of the twentieth century, geriatric training was not a field that many doctors took an interest in. This lack of education in meeting the needs of the aged will change in coming years as the proportion of elderly people in the population rapidly increases and more doctors realize that they will be faced with practices composed of mostly senior citizens.)

During Mama's last year I was finally able to obtain the services of a geriatric specialist, Dr. Hyde. Unfortunately, he was the only geriatric specialist in the area and was consequently in great demand. At one point I expressed my frustration to his nurse for his persistent failure to return my calls, and she informed me that he had fourteen hundred patients—what did I expect? What I expected was for him to be accessible to the family of a patient who could not track or participate in the particulars of her care herself. He was a doctor who had the capacity to provide appropriate care to his elderly disabled patients, but he was a doctor who was simply not there.

Accessibility, accountability, and geriatric knowledge are the most important factors to consider when selecting a nursing home doctor. In most cases, in order to get good medical care for a loved one, the family must be prepared to get actively involved. When no one is ensuring otherwise, it is often normal practice for doctors to disregard a patient's previous medical history and to prescribe medications excessively. Families should not hesitate to change doctors if they feel that better care may be available with someone else. Hopefully, if enough families are willing to make the break from inadequate doctors, a higher standard of care will be set.

Watching my mother toward the end of her life helped deepen my sense of the journey of the soul. As I sat with Mama over those long months in the nursing home and watched the slow dissipation of her physical form, I was awed by the mystery of a soul so entwined with mine and yet whose meaning I could never possibly know. I developed a profound respect for this mystery, my mother's life, and I learned to honor it for what it was. I was at last free from my notions of how her life should have been.

As part of my sense of Mama's continuing soul journey, I became aware fairly early on at the nursing home of two very tall angels, both dressed identically in white, who stood silently and ever vigilantly, one on each side at the head of Mama's bed. Let me assure you that while I consider myself spiritually inclined, even receptive, I am most certainly not given to hallucinations! Yet, somehow, the presence of these two angels, whom I saw clearly in my mind's eye, and who did not particularly look as I would have pictured angels, seemed as vivid and appropriate to me as would have two potted plants adjacent to her bed. I took great comfort in these angels. Although they seemed to pay no attention to me whatsoever, their presence reminded me that we are never as alone as we sometimes think we are.

Feeling that Mama was being looked after in a way far beyond my understanding, I was able to devote myself to each moment she and I still had together. I would sometimes mention the good times we had shared in the past so she would know how much I treasured the memories and how lucky and rich I felt to have them. But because of the stroke, Mama never again hugged me or held my hand or kissed me. Although it was an immeasurable loss, I tried not to become saddened by dwelling on the things we could no longer do. If she had not expressed her love to me so vigorously with her eyes and her words, it would have been much more difficult to handle. Even now as I write this, her eyes gaze lovingly at me from a photo near my desk.

As much as I disliked being in the nursing home, being with Mama remained a meaningful and happy experience. I would listen to her carefully, reminding myself that I needed to enter her world and not expect her to return to mine. I really tried to understand her as she was in that condition—and to be present with her whether I could understand her or not.

I began to experience an unanticipated sense of liberation. Since Mama no longer remembered the past except in disconnected bits and pieces, she did not remember the precise details of our relationship. We were, for the first time in our lives, free of our "roles" of mother and daughter. What was left? Pure love. Never once did I enter Mama's presence, whether after an absence of a few minutes or a few months, without her recognizing me as someone she loved. When I was with Mama, it was as though the past and the future no longer existed. Everything had evaporated but the two of us in that moment.

I remember Mama asked me once, "Now, why is it that I love you?"

"Oh, because I'm your daughter, I guess," I replied breezily.

"Oh, yeah," she affirmed.

That was it, and that was enough. It wasn't because I was this way or that way, or had done this thing or that thing. Mama loved me simply because I was her daughter, and I loved her because she was my mother. Reason enough, and irrevocable.

As precious as every day of her life was to me, I still dreaded the possibility of Mama going on for years and years in a nursing home. As Mama had begun to age and consider what might lie ahead, she had often adamantly expressed that she did not want to become dependent, and she hoped she would not live long enough for it to come to that. Alas, she had lived long enough to become extremely dependent. Determining what was best for her while she was in the nursing home was neither obvious nor simple. It seemed that all the choices her family had to make for her were between bad and worse. We *never* got to choose between two *good* choices, and sometimes we didn't have any choices at all.

We naturally wanted to protect Mama from all the suffering we could, which necessitated keeping her as well as possible. The right thing seemed to be to support her life force until it concluded of its own accord. However, the line between comfort and life-prolonging measures is intrinsically not a clear one. With the exception of the hospice movement, most medical orientations have not gone far in clarifying that line. My conviction grew that prolonging Mama's life deliberately in any way seemed as futile and unconscionable as did hastening her demise.

Just four months after Mama's stroke, I received a call from an unfamiliar doctor who was filling in for Dr. Short while he was away on vacation. The doctor informed me that my mother was bleeding internally, that her blood count was dropping rapidly, and that she probably had only a few days to live. Panic and distress gripped me as I wrestled with thoughts of my mother's death. Then a calmer, by then familiar feeling came over me. I felt pretty sure that the end had yet to come and Mama's death was not imminent. This time, though, I was compelled to be with her through the emergency.

With travel arrangements quickly made, I was soon striding briskly through the shiny, linoleum corridor of the nursing home, drawing a deep breath only when I was at her side. As always, it was a happy reunion.

One of my brothers had come, too. Within a short time of our arrival, Mama's mysterious internal bleeding stopped and her blood count returned to normal. The crisis had passed. Given Mama's weakened condition, everyone concerned felt that it was enough to leave it at that. It was the tacit consensus that no heroic measures were to be taken with Mama. Shortly after this episode I signed the paper making Mama an official DNR patient. DNR means "Do Not Resuscitate" and is used in medical records for people who, should they experience a potentially terminal event, are to be permitted to die rather than be forcefully revived by such means as CPR, intubation, and other invasive procedures.

The bleeding episode felt like a trial run, an unsettling rehearsal for what must inevitably lie ahead. As fervently as I had not wanted my mother to have to live in a nursing home, I realized how glad I was that she was still alive. Even though Mama was helpless and at the mercy of strangers, I was still able to cling to what we had. I felt a little guilty at times that maybe it was selfish of me to want her to stay alive. Mostly, though, I treasured our relationship, standing by her and thriving on the love we shared. Ultimately, I knew it was not up to me to prolong her life or to let it end. It was only up to me to be there with Mama as best I could.

9
TO EAT OR NOT TO EAT

When you have to make a choice and don't make it,
that is a choice.
William Blake

MAMA HAD NO SOONER survived her close call
with death than we received the unexpected news that
she may have regained the ability to swallow. The speech
therapist would need to perform a test first to be sure.
The procedure would involve inserting a tube with a tiny
camera at the end of it through Mama's nose and into
her throat to observe whether her swallow reflex was
functioning. Even as we labored over the decision to do
this invasive test, we felt we could not say no. How could
we deny Mama the opportunity to eat, to recover some
small measure of normalcy, and to escape having her
nourishment poured directly into her stomach? Assured
that it would be a one-time, brief, and painless event that
could be done in her room, we decided the procedure
was worth it if it paved the way for Mama to be able to
eat again.

I was naturally gladdened by this prospect for Mama, hoping that being able to eat would be a source of pleasure for her and would provide some interruption in the monotony of her days. I also anticipated that it would be a way for me to do something for her by bringing her treats and feeding her myself when I was there. Even so, the news was not met without some concern. Although Mama might be able to swallow, she would now be at high risk for aspiration, having food enter her lungs via her windpipe. To minimize this danger, Mama's food would have to be puréed, and special feeding instructions would need to be followed by those who fed her.

The possibility of aspiration was a life-threatening complication, and it worried us tremendously. I knew that with high staff turnover, poor communication, and the tendency for carelessness, there would be a lot of room for error. The speech therapist's faith that all would go smoothly was as strong as my doubt. She assured us that she would personally train the staff and keep a watchful eye over them to ensure that Mama was fed correctly.

Seeing Mama fed through the G-tube had always bothered me. It was so impersonal. The nurses just poured the contents of a canned milkshake into the tube as fast as they could, in a hurry to get on to their other duties. I imagined it would be uncomfortable to have something enter the digestive system all at once like that, without even the pauses that sips and swallows would provide. If food were meant to go into a body all at once, why would we be structured the way we are?

Why would we be able to swallow only small quantities at a time?

The G-tube also had to be flushed regularly with water to keep it clean. One time I witnessed a nurse, presumably to save herself the few steps to the bathroom for tepid water, use the ice water from the container that was perfunctorily placed next to Mama's bed every day. (Despite the fact that Mama couldn't drink anything, ice water was always placed by her bed. It is one of those government regulations in which good intentions have gone awry.) The nurse proceeded to spill some of the water as she poured it. A few moments later when an aide came in, the nurse apologized to the aide for spilling water onto the pillowcase, thus requiring it to be changed. After the nurse left, I discovered that she had actually spilled the ice-cold water onto Mama's shoulder and the shoulder of her nightgown, and yet she had not bothered to apologize to Mama. The episode conjured up the all too familiar feeling that Mama just wasn't a person to some of the staff.

After the speech therapist completed the test on Mama's throat, Mama was deemed capable of swallowing and was put on a puréed diet. Even though the G-tube would stay in place should Mama ever need it again, I felt as though we had *gained* some ground for a change, had met with a victory at last. Yet a dark cloud of foreboding lurked in the back of my mind. I worried that Mama wouldn't be fed correctly and would aspirate.

In spite of my reservations, I tried to relish this new development in Mama's condition. She would have a variety of meals three times a day and could join the other residents on her ward in the dining room at meal times. I was glad for this change in Mama's social situation because I thought that Mama would be glad. I knew she often seemed to perk up when other people were around, especially if they paid attention to her or tried to include her in conversation. Unfortunately, I failed to consider how seldom such exchanges would take place in a nursing home dining room filled with total care residents like Mama. In the long run, I hope that having a change of scenery and other faces to look at provided Mama with at least some diversion.

Initially I was disappointed when Mama seemed indifferent to what she ate. Food had always been a subject that interested her. I tried to elicit enthusiasm in her puréed meals, commenting on smells, speculating on tastes, pointing out items I thought she might especially like. Bananas had been a favorite food of hers, but she didn't seem too impressed when I mashed up fresh ones for her. I realized her sense of taste was probably greatly diminished.

Although Mama's zeal for food may have been lacking, she readily responded to the activity as a social occasion, which she had not had the opportunity to do with the brief tube feedings. She appeared to enjoy the interaction, playing along and responding positively to my *bon apétit* urgings. It was a time that I could share with her, and I tried not to think of what it would be like for her once I had gone, with aides mechanically scooping food into her mouth.

Mama's nursing home life consisted of being either in her bed or in her "geri-chair," a vinyl-covered recliner with wheels. The latter gave us both a break from her normal routine, since it provided us with some mobility. I often took advantage of mild weather to take Mama outside. She seemed to enjoy these excursions, which had a remarkably calming effect on her almost immediately. I would get Mama's sunglasses from her drawer and say, "Hang your shades on your nose, Mama, and we'll blow this place." She always smiled at that. I'd put the sunglasses on her, and with her looking as jaunty as a movie star, I'd wheel her down the corridor. Just for a moment I'd let myself believe that we were really going somewhere. We'd just get into my car, drive away, and never come back. Sometimes the fantasy would tiptoe away quietly, and I'd be left feeling contented, sitting on a bench in the open air with Mama in her chair next to me. Other times some insolent inner voice would coldly remind me that I couldn't even lift her in and out of her chair by myself, let alone take her someplace in my car.

The grounds of the nursing home were sparse and closely clipped but relatively pleasant. The lawn was a little barren, but there were some small ornamental trees about, a few flowers here and there, and an artificial pond out front. It was blessedly quiet, except for the sounds of the birds and the humming of the air conditioners. Mama almost always promptly fell asleep whenever I took her outside, which made me feel like she was missing the experience. But I came to realize that her response suggested she must have felt soothed and relaxed being out there. I remember one spring day sitting in the sun next to Mama when I, too, became drowsy. I let my head fall forward and my jaw slacken, just like Mama's and the other old folks' did when they napped, and I dozed off. Not only did I enjoy sharing a nap with Mama like that, but it turns out it is a fairly pleasant way to snooze. I had to chuckle to myself later, imagining what a sight it must have been for those who passed by.

I wish someone could have taken Mama outside more often. It was not the sort of thing the staff found time for, however, and Aunt Margaret couldn't manage the chair.

The aphasia that occurred after Mama's stroke often foiled her attempts to communicate. It was frustrating to have to guess at what she was thinking, especially since it was obvious she was thinking about something. Mama would get very agitated, clearly frustrated that she couldn't make herself understood and undoubtedly angry that she was in such a circumstance in the first place. She would sometimes vocalize her agitation with her situation by railing at me, her caregivers, or no one in particular. At such times her attitude could take a combative turn, putting me in the position of apologizing feebly because I simply couldn't comprehend what was upsetting her. Sometimes she would exhort me to "do something." Those were difficult moments for me, since I so much wanted to do something to help her but had no idea what else I could do.

While it is appropriate to comfort someone in such a state, it isn't helpful to deny how they feel. I knew there was a big difference between commiserating with Mama—telling her I was sorry she was feeling the way she was feeling—and ignoring her situation—telling her that everything was fine and she should stop expressing such feelings. I told Mama repeatedly how sorry I was that she was having to go through this experience and how much I wished I could make it different. She would eye me carefully when I made such statements. I can only hope she felt understood and less alone with her predicament.

The nurses, and especially the aides, seemed irritated by Mama's ornery moods. I tried to elicit empathy from them, not only for Mama but for all the residents of the nursing home. I tried to get the staff to see how difficult it was for the residents and how they needed to let off steam in some way. But I never felt as though I succeeded in getting Mama's caregivers to see any but their own points of view.

Mama also expressed her agitation physically with the almost constant, often rhythmic movement of her right arm. Sometimes I would think she was sleeping, but then her arm would start moving, and I would know she wasn't altogether resting. I have since learned that repetitive movement like Mama's is known to be a way of coping with the boredom and anxiety of confinement. It has also been observed in species as diverse as primates, birds, and fish. Most of us have experienced boredom or anxiety-producing situations in which we calm ourselves by drumming our fingers or wiggling a foot back and forth. For people who are in some way paralyzed, any movement they can muster serves as both a comfort and a means of expression.

Scratching herself and rhythmically banging or shaking her bed rails with her right hand were Mama's most frequent activities. The staff probably wouldn't have given the actions a second thought, except that she was tearing her fragile skin with all the scratching. Without stopping to consider or address what might lead Mama to act in such a manner, the head nurse had ordered that Mama's right hand be placed in a mitt.

Despite the paralysis along her left side, Mama had apparently been adept at removing the mitt, out of the sight of the staff. The only reward for Mama's cleverness, however, was a tighter restriction. A wrist cuff was fitted so that her hand could be tied to the bed rail by the two strings attached to it. Although the cuff's strings were long, the nurses and aides tied Mama's wrist so close to the rail that her arm was effectively immobilized. Although I did not want to see Mama scratch herself raw, the cruelty of tying her up like that was unbearable.

I thought it must surely be illegal, but when I investigated, I learned that government regulations permitted it. Disabled and disoriented residents of nursing homes are routinely tied to chairs and beds. The nursing home industry likes to demonstrate progress by citing statistics—such as that since 1995 use of physical restraints in nursing homes is down from 38 percent to 15 percent. While that is undeniably good news, for the 15 percent of nursing home residents who are still being restrained, my guess is that those statistics are of little consolation. The validity of such a statistic becomes quite ambiguous, too, unless we can compare it to the rate of use of chemical restraints, i.e., how many of the 23 percent released from physical restraints were just put on a tranquilizer instead?

The regulations were originally created with the residents' welfare in mind, but the restraints often do more harm than good. No physical restraints is ultimately the only acceptable goal. We have to believe we don't have to tie up elderly human beings.

I flashed back to a similar situation at one of the nursing homes I worked in as a nurse aide. An octogenarian resided there who was considered an escape artist. Because she was no longer strong enough to walk but insisted on trying, and because she had the tendency to slump and slide while sitting, she was placed in a vest with long straps that were tied to her chair to help keep her in place. She passionately resented the restraints and used Houdini-like dexterity to emancipate herself, resulting in her simple vest being upgraded to what was in effect a straitjacket, binding her arms and trunk to her chair. In a shrill tone that echoed through the halls, she would often cry out again and again, "Get me out of here!" (the ubiquitous sentiment of nearly every person I have ever met who resided in a nursing home). When the woman fell silent for too long, it was a signal to investigate. The aides would find her not only out of her restraints but often completely out of her clothing as well, sprawled somewhere nearby, her wasted muscles having betrayed her escape.

I could appreciate the staff's dilemma regarding Mama's scratching herself, but I could not stand by with Mama's only mobile limb denied movement. I told them they would have to find another solution. Period. Happily, Mama eventually solved the problem herself by using the pads of her fingertips instead of her nails to scratch her skin.

I shudder to think of the poor residents who don't have any advocates to stick up for them as I could for Mama in this case. However, it doesn't have to be this way. When doctors and nurses make a greater effort to understand the people in their care, they are able to come up with solutions that work for everyone.

It had been an unusually eventful visit—rushing to Mama's bedside as she seemed to be bleeding to death, only to have her promptly recover and in fact regain the ability to swallow—and it was the only time I ever left the nursing home feeling any sense of triumph. Mama had regained a small degree of normalcy in being able to eat, and I had felt the great satisfaction of throwing her arm restraint into the wastebasket. I know I probably should have returned it to the nurses station, but I couldn't bear the thought of it being used on some other hapless elder. No one ever asked me what happened to it.

10

FINDING OUR WAY

I don't know about life. You live so long and you get
used to it. And then it slips away . . . and then what
do you do?
Mama, August 1993

WHEN MAMA WAS first admitted to the nursing
home, she was enrolled in the standard therapy sessions
for victims of stroke—a busy schedule of physical, occupational, and speech therapy exercises. After a prescribed
number of weeks, however, the various therapists determined that Mama had not made enough progress to
justify further payment from Medicare, and she was
dropped from the rehabilitation departments' rosters. It
seems she had frequently fallen asleep during her sessions throughout the day.

Poor Mama. There she was, eighty-five years old,
having endured a total upheaval in her health, lifestyle,
and personal environment, and now she was being
penalized for sleeping! Most of the literature concerning
recovery for stroke victims emphasizes beginning some
form of rehabilitative therapy as soon as possible follow-

ing an incident. However, the literature also indicates that too much therapy—or pressure—too soon can actually be counterproductive. Given Mama's age and the fact that she had recently undergone major surgery (which is not the case with many stroke patients), it might well have been more useful to have allowed Mama to begin therapy after she had regained more of her strength.

Once Mama was dropped from the therapy sessions, no further efforts were made on the part of the nursing home to assist her in regaining any of the ground that was lost due to the stroke. From then on, her care was strictly physical maintenance. Unfortunately, once Medicare coverage runs out and a person without private funds becomes a Medicaid patient, there is no further reimbursement for therapy. Consequently, we will never know how much Mama might have recovered if she had been given the opportunity.

Months later, physicians' evaluations typically described Mama as alert, responsive, able to answer simple questions, and demented. According to *The 36-Hour Day* (Mace, et al.), a helpful guidebook for caregivers of Alzheimer patients, *dementia* is the term chosen by the medical profession as "least offensive and most accurate" for describing the wide range of conditions that make up cognitive impairment. Given the word's long association with craziness and insanity—synonyms still found in the dictionary—the notion that it is not an offensive word seems peculiar indeed.

To complicate matters, dementia does not refer to a static state of cognition. Although people can suddenly revert or regress to a higher or lower functioning level within the limits of their dementia, they are generally classified according to only their lowest level of functioning. This approach does not encourage caregivers or medical personnel to expect or even try to elicit the highest functioning behavior possible. It is typical to think, well, so-and-so doesn't know what is going on, so why try to reach her? Applying the label of dementia becomes a way to disenfranchise people and ceases to be a way to convey useful information.

It was certainly evident to me that Mama's state was not static, particularly when she would suddenly emerge into a clearer place, however briefly. Whether she was aware all the time but could only summon the ability to respond occasionally, or whether her consciousness was vacant much of the time, with some sort of "coming to" or surfacing occurring periodically— either way her presence was much too valuable to ignore. It was as though everyone wanted to deny the moments when she behaved in a way that was incongruent with their expectations. I think that sometimes it is easier for caretakers and family members to believe that someone is hopelessly confused and unreachable than to deal with the implications that they are not. Yet time and again Mama surprised me, not only with her perspicacity, but with her creativity in finding ways to interact with me.

One time as I sat near Mama, we were gazing at one another for some time when Mama suddenly reached out and began to trace my face gently with her finger, all the while looking at me intently. It felt like such a tender, fresh seeing for her. After a while she stopped, and smiling her dear crooked grin (since the left side of her face no longer moved as much as the right side), she said, "You have nice 'whatchamacallits.'"

"Features?" I asked.

She nodded. I was so touched that it didn't dawn on me until later how unusual this occurrence had been. Although Mama had the ability to move her right arm with fairly full range, she seldom used it for anything that could be considered volitional. Her arm movements were typically repetitive and rhythmic, and while she might use her hand to rub or scratch, she rarely used it to reach for or take hold of things, except sometimes to grasp the bed rail. Nor did she ever reach for the spoon to feed herself or otherwise reach for her food, other than occasionally to touch it randomly in the way that an infant might touch something in his or her environment. An occupational therapist had mentioned to me that when she handed Mama a hair brush and encouraged her to use it, Mama just dropped it. The therapist assumed that Mama physically couldn't brush her hair, but I wondered if Mama was choosing not to brush her hair. I strongly suspect that sometimes people just plumb run out of effort. I, too, discovered that if I handed Mama something, she soon let it drop from her grasp, if she took hold of it at all.

Declining to use her right arm and hand with purpose had not only brought about the demise of Mama's occupational therapy but had convinced nearly everyone that her brain was too damaged for her to execute even the simplest of tasks. Yet that Saturday morning, when she reached out to explore my face with her fingers and then commented on the experience, proved that her cerebral functioning was still connecting mind with hand. Mama was also observed using her hand to keep time to music. Even more intriguing was when she occasionally handed me imaginary items and then instructed me to dispose of them in some way. Sometimes I was to deposit whatever it was into the wastebasket. Other times I was to place it on a shelf or in a drawer. I was always careful to obtain instructions as to what I was to do with each item without betraying the fact that I didn't know what the item was. These rituals seemed to satisfy Mama. I believe they were purposeful games, akin to role plays, that may have enabled Mama to feel like she had some control over and effect on her environment.

Some people might refuse to play along with such fantasies, feeling embarrassed or distressed by the idea that it is a further sign of their loved ones' mental failure. Yet doing so denies the aged person this opportunity for self-expression. Sometimes even the most apparently disoriented folks can give us clues about their wants and needs if we know how to look and are willing to consider unconventional ways of communicating.

One day I realized that Mama's most frequent hand motions were circular. As I watched and contemplated her movements, it occurred to me that she had been a meticulous housewife for most of her life and had no doubt spent many hours scrubbing, rubbing, and polishing things in just such a circular motion. With this realization came the recognition that the movements were not necessarily random and meaningless, as assumed by most observers.

My observations confirmed for me the necessity of trying to communicate with Mama on her own terms. I continued resisting the temptation to pull her into a mode more familiar to me, which would be an endeavor not only futile but also insensitive and inappropriate. I had to remind myself repeatedly that Mama was at a new stage in her life, and it called for a different understanding and different ways of interacting.

In my longing to find more effective methods for relating to Mama, I discovered the work of a psychologist named Arnold Mindell. Originally trained as a physicist and then a Jungian analyst, Dr. Mindell developed his own system of working with people called Process Psychology, or Process Work. Initially his work was used for accessing otherwise unconscious material from people undergoing psychotherapy. Several years ago Dr. Mindell, along with his wife and professional partner, Amy Mindell, launched a bold experiment with coma patients that resulted in some extraordinary discoveries. As good fortune would have it, the Mindells came to Santa Fe about six months after Mama's stroke occurred to do a workshop about their coma work, and I was able to attend.

First and foremost the Mindells provided me with confirmation that despite what may seem like overwhelming impairment of the channels of communication, human beings often remain accessible to interaction if we are able to find the means. By closely observing patients in comas, the Mindells discovered that the patients were still capable of making bodily gestures, such as moving their facial muscles or their fingers.

While medical personnel have traditionally assumed that these movements are meaningless twitches of the autonomic nervous system, the Mindells wondered whether, with encouragement, patients could use these motions to communicate. They began speaking gently and unintrusively to comatose people, inviting them to make contact.

I was impressed by the almost reverential respect they showed for these patients, people whose bodies had been subjected daily to the clinical handling of many strangers. The Mindells didn't so much as touch a person's wrist with the tips of their index fingers without first making their intention known verbally. After a time, they would comment when they noticed the person doing something such as raising an eyebrow or moving a finger. They would then suggest that the person perform the same movement deliberately, such as lifting the finger once if the answer to a question was "no" and twice if it was "yes," or some other system. To the amazement of family and medical personnel, comatose patients began communicating.

In some instances the contact with patients seemed to precipitate an awakening from the coma, even among patients who had been unresponsive for very long periods of time. For other patients the contact led to ending the coma, while others remained in their comatose state after showing some indication that they were pursuing a thread of consciousness that they did not wish to have interrupted. Still others seemed to resolve some issue that had been keeping them in the coma and then proceeded to die. The goal of the Mindells was never to interfere with a coma or to impose anything on the patient they were reaching out to. Instead, their intent was to offer a means of communication, and when applicable, to convey the comatose person's wishes to relatives and caretakers. I suspect that the Mindells' incredible respect for what was happening, without having any agenda or expectation that it should be a certain way, was part of the reason for their success.

The Mindells point out that there are many channels of communication, most of which people ignore due to an overriding reliance on speech. As a system, Process Work focuses on the other channels, which become critical when the speech channels are blocked, as they might be in the aftermath of a stroke or during other progressive cognitive malfunctions. In addition to the conduit that the Mindells' method provides for people in comas, the results also offer the hope to caregivers that people who are extremely withdrawn may be reached as well.

In the months following Mama's stroke, knowing that I would never accept the alternative of abandoning my attempts to communicate and letting Mama slip beyond my reach, I was compelled more than ever to find ways of communicating beyond the limited success I had already had. Although I often felt discouraged and unsure of myself, I received affirmation from the Mindells' workshop that I was actually on the right track. I gained the tools to build a conceptual framework for focusing and expanding what I was trying to do. With a lightened heart, I eagerly anticipated my next visit with Mama in the nursing home.

On that next visit, now more than six months since

the stroke, I noticed that something was shifting in Mama's attitude. I think we both were struggling less, not only with the situation in such alien surroundings but also with the communication difficulties we were experiencing. Mama seemed to be less agitated, and I felt increasingly as though I could relax and just be with her. I found myself taking a lighter, less urgent approach to talking with Mama, letting it be like a game of table tennis, except the interaction was cooperative rather than competitive. I have always thought such games would be more worthwhile if the goal were not to make the other player miss the ball but to work together to keep the ball moving back and forth as long as possible. That is how many of my conversations with Mama were. There was no goal in mind, and no overwhelming importance was assigned to the content of our interaction. It was enough just to keep the conversation going and then let it come to a natural resting point.

During this time, Mama took up the habit of counting. Whenever the staff cleaned her, dressed her, or transferred her between chair and bed, Mama counted. It is possible she did this because she found her circumstances distressing. Other times she sat there and counted probably because she was bored. In any case, I was delighted that she was able to come up with this technique to soothe herself.

Seeing an opportunity to join Mama in her world, I often accompanied her in counting. With her leading, we developed rhythms together. Sometimes she would say four numbers in sequence, and then I would say the next four in the sequence, using the same intonation and pacing as she had. She would indicate completion by stating a number emphatically, in response to which I would echo it equally emphatically, and then we would say it back and forth a few times, nodding and affirming it. Mama always seemed animated and gratified by these exchanges. The aides acted as though they thought we were nuts, but we didn't care. People need interaction with others in their environment through whatever medium they can use. We had found a new place where we could meet and communicate.

With learning gained from the Mindells, I knew that in order to further my communication with Mama, I should look carefully for any physical "signals" that Mama might send out. Then I was supposed to "go" with the signal. Watching Mama brandish her arm in the air one day, I thought about this instruction. Unlike a comatose patient whose movements are usually very subtle, here was Mama with the grand gestures of her undulating right arm. I reached out my arm to Mama's, touching her lightly, forearm to forearm. Then, without directing or inhibiting her, I just followed her lead, like a dance partner. Mama continued on, and as she got into it, a trusting rapport grew. I occasionally added some resistance for her to push against, and she loved it! We went at it for well over an hour the first time. I had to change arms, but Mama just kept going. I complimented her on the strength of her arm, and my heart swelled when I saw the glow of pride on her face. Mama wasn't being given much credit for anything in those days. I was thrilled not only to participate with her in this way but also to enable her to feel capable at something. I wondered what it looked like to passersby to see an old lady and her middle-aged daughter waving their arms around together. To us it was a dance as dynamic as Tai Chi, now yielding, then pressing, always flowing together, as graceful and delightful as any dance could be. We were finding our way in this different and unfamiliar world.

11

JUST CALL ME SISYPHUS

> What is demanded of man is not, as some existential philosophers teach, to endure the meaninglessness of life; but rather to bear his incapacity to grasp its unconditional meaningfulness in rational terms.
> *Viktor Frankl*

I ALWAYS HAD plenty to do while I was at the nursing home, all of which I tried to accomplish while Mama napped so I wouldn't miss time I could spend with her. I would go through all of Mama's clothing, refreshing name labels as needed and arranging everything neatly in her drawers and closet. I made innumerable, usually futile trips to the laundry room to try to recover missing items. Determined to hang on to the new socks I had bought her, I once wrote her name two inches high in laundry-proof ink on the bottom of each sock.

I also read through Mama's chart, scanning for anything inconsistent or otherwise of concern. I looked up her medications in the *Physician's Desk Reference* that was kept at the nurses station in order to ensure that she was not being drugged unnecessarily or excessively. I also wanted to make sure there were no contraindications that applied to her, which sometimes did occur since her doctors frequently ignored her prior medical history. Part of my exercise in monitoring these matters was to show the staff I was checking on my mother. One time a nurse tried to stop me from looking at Mama's chart, but just as I was about to read her the riot act, another nurse, who knew me and was used to my level of involvement, intervened.

Another way I was able to look out for Mama was by refusing to leave her room while nurses and aides attended to her. It is understandable that many family members feel uncomfortable seeing this sort of activity. They may also feel they are preserving their loved one's privacy by not watching. Certainly, if loved ones make it clear that they are the ones who feel uncomfortable with family members present, it is important to respect their wishes in this regard and not insist on observing.

Still, it is a great concern when nursing home residents, such as my mother, are not able to convey information about their conditions. There is often no other way to know for sure how a person is being treated or to see areas of the body that are otherwise hidden by clothing. Family members might never find out about bed sores, cuts, bruises, skin problems, or other anomalies if they don't look for themselves. Fortunately, I felt that my mother was probably comfortable with me there, since in past years she had often sought my assistance in grooming tasks as they became difficult for her to manage.

The amount of physical care Mama needed for her to maintain a decent level of health and hygiene was enormous and unceasing. She required prompt cleaning whenever she soiled herself, and the cleaning needed to be done gently so as not to damage her skin. In order to avoid aspiration, staff who fed her had to be extremely careful to feed her slowly, making sure she stayed in an upright position during and for at least thirty minutes after each meal. It was important that her head remain elevated when she lay in bed to further avoid the risk of aspiration. Staff needed to turn her frequently enough to avoid bed sores. Proper care also included putting moisturizer on her skin to maintain elasticity and comfort. Providing oral care for her teeth and gums was necessary to prevent infection. Her nails had to be kept short so that she didn't tear her skin when she scratched herself. Adjusting her when she slipped in her chair or otherwise got herself in an uncomfortable position was important. Supporting her properly during transfers prevented needless stress on her both physically and psychologically. These very basic needs formed a long but not unreasonable list. The difference between doing them right and doing them wrong (or not doing them at all) is unmistakable.

Being left too long in one position is a particular physical hazard for total care residents like my mother. It is the primary cause for the loss of circulation that leads to skin breakdown, which ultimately results in the open, bleeding wounds known as bed sores. These ghastly sores typically range from a quarter of an inch to an inch or more in diameter. They start out as red areas on the skin. If not attended to properly, there is further breakdown of tissue as the sores grow deeper and deeper, eventually going all the way to the bone. They most frequently occur in the area around the sacrum, or lower back, where, whether the person is sitting or lying down, constant pressure is most common.

Whether elders have bed sores is a good indicator of the quality of care that is being provided. Elders who can no longer move themselves must be repositioned regularly so that their body weight is not resting in any one place for too long. A head nurse on my mother's ward told me that nursing home regulations require that immobile residents be turned every two hours while in bed in order to shift their weight distribution and to vary the pressure on their body parts. If necessary, pillows can be used to position residents on their sides. But when there is a shortage of pillows, the efforts of conscientious aides who try to keep up with the necessary regimen are hampered.

In the course of a person's physical disintegration, bed sores become more difficult to prevent. When someone is very near death, subjecting them to the disturbance of repositioning can be unduly inconsiderate. However, until that point, nursing home staff need to follow the guidelines for preventing bed sores. The reality remains that in many facilities, including the one my mother was in, dependent elders are moved as little as once during an eight hour shift. Even then, most of the movements that occur are merely back and forth between bed and chair, which may not provide any relief if the weight of the body remains on the same spot. In addition, many nursing home residents are in effect lying down even when they are in their chairs, since the recliners are cranked back in order to use gravity to keep flaccid bodies from sliding onto the floor.

Other methods of preventing bed sores, such as gentle massage to stimulate circulation, are seldom employed by overworked staff in nursing homes. Although various devices can be used in chairs and beds to relieve sacral pressure—doughnut-shaped pillows, "egg crate" foam cushions and mattresses, gel-filled mattresses and pillows—these items are often in short supply in many nursing homes. A resident's personal cushion also can lie unnoticed in a closet where one staff person may have stored it and the next staff person does not rediscover it.

It distressed me a great deal to know that Mama couldn't turn herself over in bed or shift her weight in her chair without assistance. She easily could be left in an uncomfortable position for hours, unable to do anything about it. According to her last doctor, the one with geriatric training, part of the nature of Mama's condition was that she no longer felt the uncomfortable pressure or nerve stimuli that prompt the rest of us to shift our positions frequently. I hoped he was right and that Mama never felt too uncomfortable.

When immobile residents aren't being repositioned regularly, it often means they aren't being checked on frequently, either. As a result, nursing home residents have been found stuck in some very bizarre and even potentially life-threatening positions. Sometimes I would find Mama in an incredibly uncomfortable-looking posture. She would be so still, just staring, waiting, as though resigned to something she knew she was helpless to alter. On at least two occasions I know of, Mama somehow rolled to the side of her bed and wound up with her head stuck between the bed rails for who knows how long before someone found her. At the time, I was unaware of how terribly dangerous this phenomenon can actually be. I learned later that many nursing home residents have lost their lives from getting trapped in their bed rails and not being discovered in time to be rescued.

Mama also often slipped down in her chair, another typical side effect of paralysis and other conditions that impede the ability to resist gravity. It was part of the conundrum of having to be left fully upright after meals with no wherewithal to maintain the position herself. I feared that hours might go by before anyone noticed she had slumped. She could even slip all the way out of the chair and wind up injured on the floor before anyone might come to reposition her. I vividly remember one instance when I walked into Mama's room and found that she had slid so far out of her slippery vinyl recliner that only her sacrum and the back of her neck were in contact with the chair. Her chin was pressed to her chest and her legs were sticking out straight in front of her, well beyond the support of the chair's leg rest. She was staring straight ahead, her blank expression revealing little of the soul trapped in that poor old vessel.

I often wondered what Mama was thinking at those times, unsure whether she just checked out or maybe even went into some sort of trance induced by her extreme helplessness. I would notice a particularly blank expression on her face on such occasions, as well as sometimes when the aides were cleaning her, another undoubtedly unpleasant event. This common psychological response of distancing oneself in some way when under such circumstances is called dissociation. When something in life is too disagreeable, people employ defense mechanisms in order to handle the stress. What happens to the people who have to do this every day, several times a day, in order to deal with their circumstances? It is a question that needs to be addressed on behalf of all nursing home residents.

Another highly disconcerting and recurring event in Mama's life took place whenever she had to be transferred. In medical settings, to "transfer" someone is to move an immobilized person from one conveyance to another—from bed to geri-chair or wheelchair, from chair to toilet, etc., and back again. This particular aspect of caring for disabled elders is probably the most strenuous for all concerned. Those elders who cannot bear any weight on their feet are the most difficult to transfer. Even with a small person like Mama, who weighed less than one hundred pounds by the time she was admitted to the nursing home, the bulk and stiffness of the person render the process awkward.

Mama often screamed when she was being transferred, a habit that rattled many of her aides. I think she was frightened to be picked up, afraid she would be dropped or otherwise injured, which is not an unrealistic fear for someone in such impotent circumstances. To ease fears about being transferred and to limit the possibility of injury, there is an approved procedure for moving dependent residents. Two aides or nurses lift the resident along four points—the two armpits and the backs of the two knees—so that the person's weight is evenly distributed. In Mama's case, she was often transferred, whether by one aide or two, by lifting her up by her armpits only. Not only was that a very uncomfortable way to be lifted, but it also risked injury to her unsupported lower torso and limbs. Throughout Mama's stay in the nursing home I tried constantly to get the aides to use their other hand to support Mama beneath her knees. Trying to motivate them, I pointed out that Mama surely wouldn't cry out so much if they used this method. But with each subsequent visit I would see that the aides had reverted to their armpit-only transfer. Considering that Mama was probably transferred between bed and chair an average of 6 times per day, 365 days a year, it was quite an ordeal for her to endure.

There are other chronic physical care issues, albeit non-life-threatening, that are frequently left unattended to in nursing homes. For example, Mama's feet were often cold, so I bought her several pairs of socks and focused on trying to get the aides to remember to put them on her when she needed them. I shouldn't have been surprised when I realized they were putting socks on her all the time, even if her feet weren't cold. At times I would find Mama so hot that she was perspiring. It seemed like such a small thing to pay attention to—a person's skin temperature and then dressing her accordingly. Yet, such consideration was almost totally outside the bounds of the care that Mama received.

The paralysis that followed Mama's stroke and the subsequent lack of movement that ensued resulted in the contraction of her left arm and hand. During the first few months after Mama's arrival at the nursing home, a young woman came in from time to time to perform range-of-motion movements with Mama's limbs, a means for both reducing contraction and improving circulation. When the therapy was discontinued, for whatever reason I do not know, I didn't protest. The young woman had seemed so inexperienced, and Mama clearly didn't enjoy having her arms and legs tugged this way and that. I couldn't bring myself to insist on more.

Mama spent a lot of time either in bed or in her chair with her legs outstretched. Before long, her ankles became rotated such that her feet were always turned in toward one another. Knowing she would never walk again, I didn't think it made a difference how her ankles were positioned so long as there were no indications of discomfort. The color and the condition of her skin looked all right. One of the nurses told me that people's ankles naturally rotated inward once they can no longer walk. I believed her and assumed that she had probably seen it happen many times before. But when I later learned how easily this condition could have been prevented by using pillows to hold her ankles in a neutral position, I felt remorse for having left it at that. I was not aware of the stress that this rotated position placed on all of Mama's connecting joints, and probably on the bones themselves, all the way up to her hips. (To see what this is like, lie down on your back when you are in bed tonight, with your legs outstretched, and slowly rotate your ankles inward as far as they will go. Notice the sensations that occur immediately, even as far up as the small of your back. Ouch!)

Mama's skin had gotten as thin as an old shirt that's been worn and washed so many times it has become transparent and easily torn. Yet, the aides would take a terry washcloth, coarse from heavy bleaching, and scrub her as though she had been digging ditches all day. Although stimulating the skin is beneficial, their methods looked excessive. When I suggested that Mama didn't need such vigorous bathing, they humored me and washed her more gently; but I had no doubt that as soon as I wasn't available to monitor them, they returned to doing it their way.

It wasn't long before Mama developed a skin rash. Considered a redhead (though her hair was more a deep auburn), Mama always had sensitive skin, so it was not surprising that it protested the treatment it received in the nursing home. The doctors and nurses discussed prescribing medication for her, both cortisone-based pills and lotions. As usual, the medical approach was to suppress the symptom without attempting to alleviate its cause.

Aides give bed baths by bringing a plastic tub of warm, soapy water to the bed of a resident, who then gets washed down with a washcloth. To my dismay, I discovered that after washing Mama, some of the aides simply dried her off without first rinsing her skin. Others would bring fresh water for rinsing her but would still use the same sudsy washcloth. The source of

Mama's rash seemed obvious to me. When I pointed out the detrimental shortcuts, the aides countered that it was difficult to rinse her properly without getting the bed unduly wet. I suggested that they might try rinsing out the washcloth first with clean water and that if they used less soap when they filled up the plastic tub—it was usually frothing with suds—the rinsing might go more easily. They grudgingly agreed to try it, and Mama's rash soon subsided.

I also had to lobby to add moisturizing lotion to Mama's required skin-care regimen. I scrawled Mama's name in big black letters on her lotion dispenser in the hope that it would actually remain in her room. Since care supplies are seldom adequately stocked in nursing homes, staff freely "borrow" from one resident to give to another—the best solution they can find when needing something otherwise unavailable. Thanks partly to the ongoing vigilance of Aunt Margaret and the steady supply the family provided, lotion was always available. How often it was used on Mama, however, was less reliable. I bought facial moisturizer for Mama, too, but I could tell by how much remained in the jar that it was seldom applied by anyone else but me. I enjoyed rubbing the lotion onto her face. It was a chance to express the gentleness and tenderness that I felt for her, to nurture her in some small way.

It was also apparent that duties such as providing oral care were getting checked off on Mama's chart when they were not actually being performed. Her dentures had disappeared within a few weeks of her arrival at the nursing home. A nurse speculated that they were probably thrown out with her soiled laundry. Their loss, of course, did not preclude her need for oral care. One method of providing this care involves using a little sponge that is attached to the end of a stick. When dipped in water, the sponge emits a mouthwash-like substance. The sponge is then used to massage and freshen a person's mouth and gums without the need for rinsing. But like most medical supplies, these implements are ridiculously expensive and are invariably in short supply at nursing homes.

The physical care of nursing home residents is further complicated by the maladies that are endemic in today's long term care facilities, and Mama certainly wasn't immune to any of these problems. Urinary tract infections, diarrhea, congestion, dehydration, rashes, and bed sores—these ailments never seem to surprise the doctors, who attribute them to residents' advanced ages and poor physical conditions. While elders do tend to have diminished immune systems and increased susceptibility to sickness, especially when they are inactive, this knowledge should be a warning for increased preventive care rather than an excuse for the various skin, digestive, and bacterial problems that occur. These afflictions could be greatly reduced with good, consistent attention to residents' hygiene as well as to their prescribed care regimens. There should be no excuse for failing to avert the preventable.

When nursing home residents are no longer able to control the flow of their urine, they develop rashes from the prolonged exposure of their skin to the urine in their bedding and diapers. In typical fashion, nursing homes respond to the frequency of these rashes by inserting catheters into aged urethras. While reducing the need for frequent cleanup, catheters provide ideal conditions for the proliferation of infection-causing bacteria. Improperly used and monitored, as they often are in nursing homes, they can present other hazards as well. I once found that my mother had been placed in her bed lying on the tubing, which of course blocked the flow.

In addition, many elderly recipients of these contraptions, no longer constrained by subservience to authority, yank them out, causing subsequent irritation to tender tissue. After Mama suffered through several urinary tract infections, I decided that she, too, had had enough. I told the staff that I did not want any more foreign objects inserted anywhere into my mother and vetoed the further use of a catheter on her. While the doctors never seemed to question writing an order for a catheter and following it with the almost inevitable antibiotic prescription a week or two later, the nursing staff, who saw the human result of that cycle in increased bowel difficulties due to the loss of healthy intestinal flora, were more willing to break the cycle and acquiesce to my request, even though they had requested the catheter in the first place. One nurse admitted to me that she knew I was right, although overall, the staff was miffed that I expected them to keep Mama clean and dry enough to avoid further rashes.

Such medical aspects of Mama's care were never ending. I had to function as a conduit of information among the ever-changing nursing home staff, the doctor, and hospital staff whenever Mama was hospitalized for conditions such as internal bleeding episodes. It was especially important to provide the hospital staff with information because they never seemed to be notified of the particulars of Mama's health care. Once I was just in time to prevent a hospital nurse from attempting to feed Mama solid food, an act that would almost certainly have choked her.

I also had to keep trying to get Mama a diet that took into consideration her pre-existing condition of chronic colitis (inflammation of the colon). I needed to be on the lookout for cuts, sores, infections, and problems with her G-tube, so that these problems were attended to promptly, regularly, and effectively. I tried to be sure that she was not given treatments that would precipitate yet another condition requiring treatment. I checked that she was given sufficient fluids to avoid dehydration, which became a problem due to her inability to consume sufficient quantities at meal times and the unavailability of staff to provide the fluids she needed between meals.

It was very frustrating to review Mama's treatment and consider that she was in a reputable nursing home. At best, her care was tolerable, with rare instances of very good. Frequently, it was heedless, insensitive, rough, and even dangerous. Yet, I was determined to keep fighting for Mama, to keep taking yet another grievance to the head nurse, the doctor, the social worker, whomever I thought might be able to help us. There was never any question of giving up, even though overseeing Mama's care in that nursing home was truly the most demanding, frustrating, and disheartening job I have ever had.

12
There IS Somebody Home

It must be said that there is as yet no scientific proof
that the brain can control the mind or fully explain
the mind. The assumptions of materialism have
never been substantiated. Science throws no light
on the nature of the spirit of man or God.
Wilder Penfield, M.D.

It galled me again and again to witness the indifference with which so many of the nursing home staff
treated my mother. They seemed unwilling to look at
what they were doing and apparently regarded my
efforts to intervene as just so much nagging. Even those
who responded positively to my suggestions would
either soon revert to their usual methods or not be taking care of my mother any more. Between staff rotations
and people quitting, Mama never had the same caregivers for long, which deprived her of the comfort and
reassurance that familiarity and continuity could have
provided.

The unkindness that some of the aides displayed
toward Mama—and that they would behave that way
right in front of me—was not only distressing but down-
right baffling. Throughout her stay at the nursing home,

when she wasn't too ill or too sleepy to respond, Mama always had an enthusiastically friendly greeting for one and all. To me it was a reflection of the wonderful graciousness that she managed to retain throughout so much of her ordeal.

One day a young male aide came into Mama's room to attend to her. True to form, Mama called out a cheery "Hi!" when the young man approached her bed. Silence. Seconds passed. Undaunted, Mama said "Hi!" again, with no less warmth or cheer. Her voice and what she said were clear and unmistakable. Still silence. Despite my pounding heart and the fury rising in my throat, I remained calm so as not to make a scene in front of Mama. I said to the young man, "She said 'hi' to you." As though coming out of a trance, he finally uttered a dull, flat "Hello." And without another word, he proceeded to perform his duties in an efficient but perfunctory manner. Mama fell silent.

When I later saw the aide in the corridor, I questioned him about his thoughtless behavior. Vaguely apologetic, he informed me that he had a lot on his mind. I was less than sympathetic and complained about the incident to the head nurse. She shared my dismay at the aide's behavior, agreeing that professional caregivers should leave their personal problems at the door when they come to work. It was good to have her agreement, but it didn't change anything.

I winced whenever I watched aides and nurses tend to Mama without speaking to her or speak to her without looking at her. I desperately wanted them to act in a manner that was kind, civil, and respectful. I knew what a difference it would make for Mama if they took a moment to explain what they were going to do and if they made an effort to listen to her, responding as much as possible to what she indicated.

All nursing home residents have psychological, emotional, and social needs regardless of their conditions. They need eye contact and whatever else seems appropriate to foster a feeling of connection and respect for their basic humanity. The lack of such behavior constitutes an assault on the human spirit and is, in many ways, the most painful offense for people to bear. It wounds more deeply than the discomfort and indignity of poor physical care.

Aides frequently scowled and scolded Mama whenever she was difficult, and I rarely heard them compliment her or thank her when she cooperated. This oversight was particularly grievous since she had so little opportunity for positive reinforcement or for being allowed the chance to feel good about herself. Wretched at the sight of how frightened she became whenever lifted from chair to bed or vice versa, I was constantly mystified by the aides' apparent unwillingness to recognize her fright. Her shrieks seemed to annoy them in the way that unpleasant noises are annoying, yet I seldom saw them reassure her or attempt to address the obvious fear that was prompting her protests. I agonized that the staff simply saw her as a helpless old lady who was too confused to know what she meant or to convey what she felt.

I was very pleased one day when Mama was being cared for by two aides who seemed considerate and attentive. I decided to take advantage of the occasion, and I suggested that they take a moment before transferring Mama to ask her whether she was ready to be moved. They agreed to try it. When they first asked her if she was ready, Mama, who apparently grasped the opportunity at hand, told them no. The aides waited patiently and about fifteen seconds later they again asked Mama if she was ready. She said yes, and they were able to move her without her crying out. Mama clearly relished being able to compose herself for a moment as well as feeling she had at least a little control over what was happening to her. But by my next visit, these aides had vanished, and I never saw any others attempt to extend such courtesy.

One day, in an obvious effort to be understood, Mama indicated by rubbing her forehead and making a face that she was experiencing an unpleasant sensation. When I asked her if her head was bothering her, she confirmed that it did. I found a nurse and asked her to come see what might be wrong. Mama started saying the word *packice*. The nurse ignored her, but I kept repeating, "Packice?" in an effort to show her that I was trying to understand. Frustrated, Mama kept saying it, louder and more urgently, the way people tend to do when they are desperate to be understood but unable to think of another way to get through. Suddenly, it dawned on me what Mama meant.

"Ice pack!" I exclaimed. "Is that what you mean? You want an ice pack for your head?"

"YES!" she roared. Mama was understood that

time for sure, but so many other times she wasn't, mostly because people didn't find the time to try.

I took some small comfort when I observed some of the nurses and aides attempting to be kind, even though their efforts were often condescending. They talked to Mama and the other residents as though they were children, cooing at them and calling them silly, saccharin-sweet names. It is the kind of thing, alas, that we often do when attempting to be affectionate toward someone who we think can't understand us. I lapsed into some form of it myself more often than I like to admit.

Mama had always been a fun person to bring presents to because she was so appreciative of whatever she was given. Of course, there weren't that many things she had use for after the stroke, and living in the small space of half a room in a nursing home didn't invite more clutter. Still, I liked bringing her what I could: clothes, socks, face cream, a new hair brush—practical things that she usually needed anew each visit. It was a way to feel as though I was doing something for her, stones tossed at the mountain of helplessness, but something nonetheless.

Like many other relatives of nursing home residents, I was always on the search for the perfect nursing home clothes—outfits that were comfortable, easy to get on and off, not too warm or too cool, and that held up under harsh and frequent laundering. Sweatpants, sweatshirts, and housecoats often won the day. I would ask Mama before I went out shopping if there was something she would like me to bring her, but she would never ask for anything. Until one day, when I told her I was going to get her a housecoat, she said she wanted a pink one. I can promise you I would not have rested until I found pink! It turned out I found a pink housecoat, the only one on the rack, in Mama's size, at the first place I stopped.

For the most part, though, Mama did not seem to care about material things anymore. I could have brought in all her "gifts" and just put them away, and she probably would not have noticed. Nor do I think that Mama remembered what I had brought her for more than a few minutes after the fact. But none of that mattered to me. What did matter was the social interaction, and I did not waste any opportunities. I always made a show of displaying the things I brought for her, holding them up one at a time, mentioning the virtues of a particular pair of socks or pointing out that I had selected her favorite brand of cold cream. Mama responded to each offering with enthusiastic approval. It was our ritual, and we each played our parts flawlessly.

In theory, all nursing home residents, regardless of how impaired they may be, are supposed to engage in recreational activities. Most facilities have activities directors whose responsibility it is to organize and provide these services. However, total care residents are frequently left out of the arrangements because they have limited abilities to participate in the activities or express their feelings about them, and so it is assumed that they are not interested in what is going on around them. Medical personnel and often the public in general tend to associate language alone with cognition and draw the conclusion that if a person cannot *say* what she wants, then she must not *know* what she wants.

This is a false assumption. Recent studies of pre-language children as well as studies of other species such as chimpanzees and gorillas indicate that thought occurs without language. Evidence also abounds that in nursing home, hospital, and closed-care settings, people whose ability to communicate verbally is impaired can still respond by other methods. In his insightful book on the emotional lives of dogs, *Dogs Never Lie About Love*, Jeffrey Masson writes of his visits to an old folks home:

> In a reversal of domestication, dogs are now being used in nursing homes, in homes for the elderly, in psychiatric hospitals and in individual therapy as a means to draw patients, the elderly and children out of isolation or depression by interacting with dogs. . . . I sometimes take my three dogs . . . to the back ward, where the most severely disabled people live. . . . On one visit, . . . [a]n old man, also "demented," could only clap his hands over and over again. He saw [my dog] and immediately reached out and patted her, totally appropriately, as if he had been doing it every day. Dogs used in this way for therapy often bring about surprising results, and lead one to wonder if the very notion of dementia might not need to be rethought.

When it comes to elderly people with mental impairments, there is a widespread belief that awareness of thoughts and feelings has become as scarce as bodily control. No distinction is made between the brain and the mind. Yet, enough is known today to ascertain that the ability to perceive is different from the ability to express oneself and that a lack of expression does not automatically mean there is no perception. Most of us cannot begin to understand what it is like to be alive but trapped in a body, or a mind, that no longer works in normal ways. Most people who are so trapped do not, or cannot, tell. Those lucky ones who have recovered from brain injuries often speak of tremendous anxiety and frustration. Some have reported that their thoughts were quite coherent; they simply could not translate them into speech. Others reported that their thoughts were quite muddled, *but they were aware of their impaired ability to think.*

We need, at the very least, to extend the benefit of the doubt to those who can no longer operate the usual channels of communication. Despite whatever impairments to functioning may exist, can we afford to ignore the possibility that awareness remains? Even if loved ones only understand what we say ten percent of the time, it is likely to be so valuable to them as to make it well worth continuing. How would you hope to be treated if it were you?

An aide mentioned to me once that she had been in the dining room with Mama when someone began to play the piano. Mama apparently became energized and demonstrated her enjoyment by smiling and waving her hand in time to the music. I was thrilled and reported it to the activities director. I begged her and the nursing staff to include Mama in any such musical activities in the future. Although all concerned responded with enthusiastic promises, I saw no indication that there was ever any follow-through.

Although a radio is not as stimulating as live music, I thought Mama would enjoy having one in her room. She had a television but didn't seem to pay much attention to it. She probably was not able to see or hear it well enough, let alone follow a program. Listening to the radio seemed much more within her reach, so I asked Mama if she wanted one. "Yes, I do!" was her prompt response. The glitch, of course, was getting the nursing home staff to turn it on, much less keep it on a station that Mama would enjoy. I let the staff know that Mama liked easy-listening or classical music, but I would often find her radio tuned to a rock-and-roll or country-and-western station—clearly the preference of someone on the staff.

One afternoon I wheeled Mama into the dining room, which was empty at the time, and began to play the piano for her. I knew that she had a definite preference in music, favoring what she called "pretty" music—music strong on melody. My style of playing on the other hand is, shall we say, abstract. I don't know how to play any actual songs, but I can do some interesting improvising. So I would play for a few minutes and then stop, looking at Mama expectantly. Mama, who looked as though she wasn't paying attention, would emphatically call out, "Nope." This response persisted for about six of my selections. Although I wasn't playing something that Mama liked, I knew that she was listening, by golly, and expressing her opinion! I was delighted.

This experience provided additional proof that even though there seemed to be little that Mama responded to with obvious interest, it didn't necessarily mean that she was unaware of or unaffected by what went on around her. I was disheartened when I entered Mama's room one day to find that she had been left in her chair, facing a blank wall. I wondered how long she had been sitting there like that. Any person, no matter how young or old, can find a change of scenery refreshing. Mama certainly did every time I took her outside. A nurse told me she thought that Mama liked to be included with the other residents who spent some time out of their rooms, lined up in the ubiquitous row of geriatric recliners across from the nurses station. This area, where people come and go and talk, received a lot of traffic, so there was much to watch and hear. (I am sure it beat staring at a wall.) However, often as not, the elders stationed in the hallway were sleeping, looking stuporous, or taking the opportunity to call out for help to anyone who passed by. It seemed a poor substitute for providing them with a genuinely stimulating activity.

From time to time, a doctor, someone on staff, or a visiting family member would make an attempt to engage Mama conversationally. She often seemed to enjoy such contacts very much. On one occasion there were several of us in her room, squeezed around her on the edges of her bed and in chairs purloined from the day room. Although she could not keep up with the pace or follow the thread of the conversations or participate in them as others did, she was plainly trying to be a part of what was going on by giving everyone smiles and looking at each person as he or she spoke. I tried to include Mama in the things we were talking about, but my efforts were either politely tolerated for a few seconds or simply ignored. While I was glad to see Mama so obviously enjoying herself, I felt anguish at how left out she might have felt. She might as well have been invisible.

People who have the same impairments as Mama's or who for other reasons cannot focus their attention or interact by usual methods are often quick to be excluded socially. Sometimes family members and caretakers find it easier to think that loved ones are unaware, because then they won't be haunted by wondering whether their loved ones are aware of any suffering. Sometimes, too, believing them to be unaware provides relief from their own discomfort of trying to relate to someone who is unresponsive or doesn't seem to make sense. It is not unusual for a family to stop visiting their relative when they believe the person no longer recognizes them. This kind of abandonment is heartbreaking, and I say this to all who have felt justified in such a rationale: Your loved ones may not seem to know who you are, *but you always know who they are!*

At one nursing home where I worked, I helped care for a woman with a rapidly progressing case of Alzheimer's. She had a large and loving family who had relinquished her to the facility with great regret. One evening I could hear talking and laughter coming from her room where several family members had gathered to visit with her. Later as I saw them filing out, I noticed they all were smiling and clearly heartened. When I went in to help the woman to bed, I commented that it sounded like she had been having a very nice evening. "Yes," she said, "I did have a good time. Those were lovely people. Who were they, anyway?" I realized right then and there that it didn't matter. They knew who they were, they knew who she was, and they had all made each other happy.

It takes effort, patience, skill, and time to relate to someone who cannot communicate by the usual means. Denying the capacity of cognitively impaired people to understand what is going on around them lets a door slam shut on further attempts at finding ways to reach them. I implore everyone who has any contact with someone who is suffering from cognitive impairment to reach out to them. If you feel like you don't know how, don't give up until you find a way.

As a culture we have a responsibility to recognize that the oldest among us, no matter how disoriented, are valuable. All elders deserve consideration for this little understood stage of life that they are going through. We need to educate ourselves and learn whatever it takes to keep them included in our personal lives and in the life of the community. It takes creativity and an open mind to discover more of these non-conventional ways of communicating. Our best teachers will be those who are waiting for us to reach them—our elders.

I remember sitting quietly once with Mama, lost in my own thoughts for a while, when I looked over at her and was startled by the vacant look in her eyes. It was so distant, yet I knew she was wide awake. I stared at her, trying to fathom this unsettling specter. After a few moments, peering into her eyes, I said to her softly, "Are you in there, Mama?"

"Sorta," she replied. It hung in the air while the silence resumed between us.

So maybe she wasn't "in there" in the same way that she used to be, but she was definitely there—and she knew it.

13
ON A WING AND A PRAYER

The butterfly counts not months but moments,
and has time enough.
Rabindranath Tagore

I LIKED THE FEELING of being a veteran air trav-
eler. Familiarity made each trip seem easier despite all
the inevitable sequels of hurry up and wait. Three airport
terminals, two flights, various check-this and check-that
counters, a shuttle or two, a few moving sidewalks, and I
would finally be in a rental car en route to Mama's nursing home. Altogether it took me about eight hours to get
from my house to Mama's bedside.

I made a mid-winter visit to see Mama a few
months after she resumed eating. It was bitterly cold in
Indianapolis that January, and I hadn't brought my heavy
coat from Santa Fe since it was such a nuisance on
the airplane. I borrowed a jacket from Aunt Margaret
(though she would have had to live at the North Pole to
own a coat warm enough for me!). Walking into the
nursing home chilled me further, with its colorless,

unyielding surfaces and angles, and the feeling of being cut off from the rest of the world once the double doors closed behind me.

I usually hurried through the halls, running a gauntlet of beckoning elders who beseeched me to do everything from put them to bed to take them home. Once when I politely declined such a request by an elderly woman standing in her doorway—I explained that I was a visitor, not a staff person—she replied, "Just pretend I'm your mother."

With mumbled apologies, I hurried away, over-whelmed at the prospect of considering any of these old ladies as I would my mother, yet sheepishly admitting to myself that she was right. I was reminded of a common admonishment in Buddhism, a faith that accepts reincar-nation, to treat all people as though they are your moth-er because they no doubt were at some time or another. Whether that is the case or not, as a society, shouldn't we aspire to treat all our elders as our mothers and fathers? And then, echoing another faith, honor them?

Everyone was in the dining hall, so I went to find Mama there. I scanned the crowd of white-headed, bony bodies scattered about the room, looking for the one that belonged to me. It was a long moment before I spotted her at a table near the windows, and I rushed to her side. To my dismay, I found her lying back about as far as she could go in her geri-chair, being fed by a somnambulant aide. Refraining from bawling out the aide, I straight-ened Mama up from this dangerous position and took over the feeding myself. I commented to the aide, in what I hoped was a reasonably courteous tone, that my mother must always be fed sitting upright in order to avoid aspiration. Obviously glad enough to have one less mouth to spoon purée into, the aide muttered that she knew of no such requirement and turned her back to me. There were several other aides as well as nurses in the dining room. Some of them *must* have known the danger of feeding Mama in such a prone position, yet no one had intervened if they had even noticed.

When I reported the incident to the nursing director and the speech therapist, who had promised to train aides personally in the proper feeding technique for Mama, I received apologies and promises that rang hollow, doing little to reassure me that the information about Mama's feeding procedure would be relayed in the future. I felt the desperation of fighting yet another battle with little hope of winning the war.

By my next visit in early spring I became more doubtful about the quality of care Mama was receiving. First, I walked in on a ridiculously clumsy attempt by a very young aide to dress Mama. The aide was trying to force Mama's paralyzed arm to unbend. She was also trying to peel open her relentlessly curled fingers. This was all in order to get Mama's arm into the sleeve of her blouse. The ludicrous aspect of the episode was that the aide had already put Mama's *normal* arm into its sleeve. I pointed out to the aide as tactfully as I could that it might be easier to dress my mother if the blouse were put on her immobilized arm first. She looked at me stonily but complied.

The next incident was more alarming, even though the two young aides showed remorse and impressed me with their air of kindness and concern. They were transferring Mama from her bed to her chair when she cried out very loudly and sharply. Her crying out was not an unfamiliar occurrence, and like most aides they ignored her. But I could tell that her cry was much more urgent in tone than usual and sounded to me as though she were in pain. I sprang toward her from the other side of the bed and discovered that they were dragging her paralyzed leg behind her. It was literally bent backwards in a manner that even a fairly agile, young person would have found uncomfortable and that Mama certainly found intolerable. The situation was compounded by the fact that the aides had not pulled the geri-chair up close enough to the bed, and so they were hauling Mama by her armpits several feet from her bed to where the chair was parked. Apologetically the aides quickly repositioned her and got her into the chair.

It made me feel terrible to have something so unthinking and dangerous happen right in front of me. I thought that maybe I should instruct every aide who walked into Mama's room, every time, how to transfer her properly. Yet, I feared that if I did, they would see me as unbearably critical and controlling, and they might treat Mama with even less sympathy. I tried to avoid antagonizing aides by taking my concerns directly to the supervising nurses. I was also careful to avoid directing a complaint against any one aide except in the most egregious cases. Some of the nurses seemed truly to appreciate my feedback, and I believe they were committed to improving the quality of care. Regretfully, I seldom saw any of them again because they usually had moved on by the time I returned.

A few weeks later, I received a call at home from a nurse who told me that Mama's paralyzed arm had a deep cut on it and required stitches. It would mean another trip to the hospital in an ambulance. I wondered what Mama thought when strange men suddenly appeared, lifted her onto a gurney, strapped her in, and wheeled her away. I noticed on previous occasions that the ambulance attendants were very courteous to her, introducing themselves and explaining what they were doing, and she responded to them in kind. (I wondered, if ambulance attendants are trained to do that, why aren't nursing home staff?)

Dr. Klink was Mama's physician at the time, and his zeal in such a situation was welcomed. He expressed indignation toward the nursing home and promised he would investigate the matter. Two days later, in a much subdued tone, he reported to me that the cut had been determined an "accident" and that no one was to blame. I had a little trouble believing that. I was told that her arm was cut while she was being given a biweekly, full bath (as opposed to her daily bed bath) in the shower room down the hall. Based on my own experiences with bathing immobilized, fragile bodies, I knew what a difficult job it could be to maneuver a resident into a shower chair and administer a bath. I also know how frustrated and impatient an aide can become in such a situation.

Several different scenarios arose in my mind as I grasped for some explanation as to how Mama may have received her injury. I wondered if Mama had been scalded by a careless aide, causing her to cry out and perhaps resist in what little way she could, and she was cut in the ensuing struggle. Or maybe Mama was nearly spilled onto the floor, and someone tried to stop her from falling—someone with a hand with too-long nails that shot out too quickly and scratched her thin skin deeply, or maybe the hand was too late and Mama fell against some sharp edge. I knew the worst possibility was that someone had cut her deliberately, but I felt more strongly that it was the result of someone's negligence.

I'll never know, though, because the aide involved never told the story. She denied having any idea how the cut, which was more than two inches long and was deep enough to require stitches, had happened. The doctor, the nursing home, and the Indiana State Department of Health, which later investigated, all accepted the aide's non-explanation and maintained that no wrongdoing had been done. I wanted to believe them, of course. But not knowing for sure has tormented me ever since, and I remain uncertain as to whether someone knew what really took place and our family was duped.

Just one week after Mama's arm was cut, I received another urgent call from a nurse, this time to tell me that my mother had suffered a broken leg. I was stunned by this news, especially after hearing that it was the femur of her paralyzed leg that was fractured. This was a leg that could only be moved by someone else. I was told that the problem was discovered when a night nurse found Mama lying in bed moaning in pain. On examining her, the nurse found an area of Mama's thigh swollen and red. No one at the nursing home admitted having any idea what could have caused the break.

Initially, Dr. Klink expressed outrage and told me that he did not intend to stand for his patients being poorly treated. But by the next day, he was again assuring me that no wrongdoing had occurred, based on the claims of the nursing home staff. He told me that this fracture of the largest bone in the human body, in a limb that in Mama's case was not able to bear any weight, had occurred "spontaneously."

I wanted to believe what he was telling me. He was the expert, the professional. I certainly did not want to believe that careless or callous treatment had injured my mother so badly. Nor did I want to make trouble where there might not be any. I had no more information than what I was being given, no way to prove any allegation of fault on the part of the nursing home. I didn't doubt that Mama had her share of osteoporosis by then. Yet I was haunted by the memory of that transfer just a few weeks earlier when the same leg had been dragged behind her in such a way that, had I not been there to intervene, the bone could have broken then and there. I told Dr. Klink, I told the doctor at the hospital, and I told various nurses about the dangerous transfer I had witnessed, but no one seemed willing to make a connection between one event and the other. Once again the health department investigated and presented a report that conformed to the nursing home's version of the matter. My credulity was stretched nearly to the limit. I truly did not know what to believe, except I was pretty sure that people in the custody of nursing homes should not be bleeding and breaking for no apparent reason.

The nursing home administrator worried that we were going to move Mama elsewhere. I would have liked to have gotten her out of there, but frankly, I was more afraid of her going somewhere even worse than I was afraid of her staying where she was. I naively thought that from then on, the nursing home would be on its toes, not daring to permit any further incidents. Furthermore, I did not want Mama to suffer the transfer trauma of being moved to completely unfamiliar surroundings. At least a couple of the aides there seemed fond of her, and most important, executed their duties with skill and kindness.

With Mama staying where she was, decisions had to be made about handling the fracture. It was one of the most vexing situations I had to deal with throughout the whole nursing home ordeal, largely because of a lack of cooperation and support from other family members. At first, the orthopedic surgeon's recommendation was to keep Mama's leg in a splint until the bone healed, not worrying if it healed straight since the leg would never again be used for walking. Assured by both Dr. Klink and the surgeon that the splint, by holding the bone in place, would serve to protect her against pain in the present as well as to eliminate chronic pain in the future, this course of action seemed to be the simplest, least uncomfortable, and therefore best solution.

I felt as though I had barely a moment to sigh with relief before I was informed that a follow-up examination of Mama's femur indicated that the lower portion of her bone had begun to migrate away from rejoining its upper segment; it was moving toward the outside of her thigh instead. The surgeon's expectation was that the sharp end of her broken bone would eventually pierce her skin, causing serious problems, including pain and potential infection. The only way to prevent this calamity was surgery. However, at Mama's age and in her condition, the anesthesia necessary for such an operation was a serious, life-threatening factor.

Fearing that Mama was suffering, my brothers and Aunt Margaret wanted a prompt resolution of the problem and urged for the surgery to be done immediately. I wanted to wait, however. I spoke with my mother's doctors and nurses, who assured me that the splint was holding her leg in place for the time being. The doctor insisted that the predicted outcome was inevitable, but he did allow that it would take many weeks for the bone to migrate to the point where the anticipated problems would occur. More important, I was also told that because her leg was being stabilized by the splint and because she was being moved as little as possible, she did not appear to be experiencing any pain.

Considering the risks of the anesthesia, the discomfort and pain that would surely follow the operation, and the knowledge of how much it would take out of her, I was enormously dismayed at the prospect of Mama undergoing surgery. While I didn't believe that delaying the operation would ameliorate any of those issues, I needed some time. I knew I would travel to be with Mama immediately if surgery was the best or necessary choice for her, but the doctors assured me that a couple of weeks would not endanger her or cause her to suffer. Although I had for some time been attempting to prepare myself for my mother's death, having it occur abruptly on an operating table surrounded by strangers just seemed too wrong. That alone, in my mind, made the surgery something that should not be rushed into.

For reasons that come from the place within us all that cannot be easily explained, the later time period felt much more propitious to me. Something about not rushing, not making this an emergency, seemed right. I told my brother it would be better astrologically if we waited, a premise he did not take very well. To tell the truth, I am not really well versed enough in astrology to know for sure whether my predictions were accurate, but it was the best explanation I could offer. I thought we should wait.

I unexpectedly had the opportunity during this time to send a photo of Mama, via a friend, to the East Indian saint Mata Amritanandamayi, who is considered by many East Indians and her western devotees to be an emanation of the Divine Mother. I had spent time with Ammachi, as she is known affectionately, when she was in Santa Fe, and I had been moved by her deeply spiritual and loving presence. I had no preconceived notion about the outcome of sending Mama's photo to this extraordinary woman, other than to seek her blessing in some way. I had never done anything like this before, but then again, I had never been in this kind of situation before, either. Reaching out for help in every way that I could seemed like the right thing to do. I was encouraged when my friend told me many weeks later that Ammachi had kissed the photo of Mama and blessed it at some length.

Meanwhile, my family was furious that I had delayed the surgery. They refused to have a civil conversation with me about the matter and insinuated that I was acting out of purely selfish motives. I was not deterred. Both the surgeon and Mama's doctor continued to support the timing I proposed, reassuring me that no ill effects would result.

Two weeks went by and I arrived at the hospital for Mama's duly scheduled operation. When the moment came for Mama to be wheeled away, I became scared and a little numb, but I didn't feel as though I was saying good-bye. It felt more like I was going through the motions of acting in some strange, dreamlike drama. After what seemed like just a few minutes, the surgeon appeared in the waiting room and informed me that Mama's leg appeared to have "miraculously" healed itself. He had discovered it after making the incision and had terminated the surgery and the anesthesia literally within minutes of beginning, so Mama was no longer in any danger.

As I stood there and received the news, I noticed that I felt no sense of surprise; it felt as though everything had simply fallen into place. Mama's leg was okay, and she hadn't died on an operating table surrounded by strangers. I spent the rest of the day with Mama in her hospital room, making sure that she was comfortable and that both the day and evening shifts were apprised of her feeding regimen. As soon as she had fully recovered from the brief anesthesia, she would be transported back to the nursing home. When everything had been attended to, I sat with Mama for a while and watched her sleep. Then, weary and relieved, I hobbled back to Santa Fe.

I was very humbled by all that had happened. Much of the time I felt as though good intentions were all I had going for me in my role as Mama's guardian. So many decisions had to be made with so few criteria for weighing the outcomes of different choices. Continually exhausted and distressed from having to put out one fire after another, I felt like I was being spread very thin. I was not able to step back and research each situation as I have been able to since. Even though it seemed it was all up to me at times, if I had really believed that, I think I would surely have collapsed under all the stress. Thank goodness I knew better—that it wasn't all up to me— even if I couldn't fathom the mystery behind it all.

14
FRACTURED CARE

Right from the moment of our birth, we are under
the care and kindness of our parents. And then later
in our life, when we are oppressed by sickness and
become old, we are again dependent on the kindness
of others. And since at the beginning and end of our
lives, we are so dependent on others' kindness, how
can it be in the middle that we neglect kindness
towards others?

The Dalai Lama

FOR ALL MY VERY VALID criticisms of the clumsy care that Mama endured at the nursing home, there
were a few aides who were distinctly kind, who treated
Mama gently, and who executed their duties skillfully.
These individuals were the recipients of my sincere grat-
itude. I even felt a sense of camaraderie with one aide in
particular, who stayed for several months and whom I
looked forward to seeing when I visited. When I walked
into Mama's room and found her clean and comfortable,
what a huge difference that made in how I felt, and in
how Mama seemed to feel, too. I only wish that Mama
could have been treated well each and every day during

the last days of her life. I remember the one visit when nothing was glaringly wrong the entire time I was there. I made a point of sharing my satisfaction with the director of nursing, which pleased her, too. But it was only that one time.

When I visited the nursing home, I often became aware of what Mama needed simply by noticing what was missing or what had not been done. It never would have occurred to me, for instance, that someone would need to be told to wipe people's mouths after feeding them. The staff of the nursing home, who had never known Mama any other way than how she was after the stroke, perhaps could not comprehend how heartrending it was for our family to walk into her room and find her sitting there, long after meal time, with dried food smeared around her mouth, attracting flies that crawled all over her face and lips. It was incomprehensible to me that the staff would not have the common decency to honor Mama's—or anyone's—dignity and wipe her mouth after feeding her.

The natural process of decline as well as the insufficient care that Mama received no doubt contributed to her increasing physical difficulties. Although I had hoped that Mama's being able to take food by mouth would enhance the quality of her life both physically and socially, it turned out instead to be the source of a large portion of her suffering. Not only was there the concern about *how* Mama was fed, but it soon became apparent that *what* she was fed was aggravating her chronic digestive ailments. Over the years Mama had learned to manage her symptoms by avoiding certain foods once she learned that they would adversely affect her. She could also control her symptoms by having frequent, small meals rather than fewer, large ones.

I tried to explain to Mama's various doctors, the nurses, and the dietitian that my mother had a history of colitis as well as diverticulosis, and that if they wanted her bowels to behave better, they needed to adhere to the same simple dietary limitations that Mama had followed. For some people, there comes a point toward the end of life when the enjoyment of eating what they please outweighs the consequences of their actions. But for Mama, who didn't seem to care what she ate, the consequences meant discomfort for her and extra work for her caretakers. Restrictions seemed both sensible and kind.

You wouldn't think it would be difficult to convince the staff that chocolate and spicy foods might not be good choices for someone prone to diarrhea. Yet it was as though neither the doctor nor the dietitian had ever seen the connection between diet and elimination. One doctor went so far as to state explicitly that there was no relationship between what Mama ate and the condition of her colon, an assertion that common sense must denounce. I would occasionally succeed in arranging a meeting with the dietitian, in which she would agree to have certain foods left off Mama's tray. Invariably, each time I returned I had to remind the dietary department of our agreement because the contents of Mama's tray would have reverted to the status quo.

Maybe to the nursing home staff and doctors this seemed like a petty battle to be fighting, as though trying to improve the bowels of an aged person who had failing digestive powers was useless. However, Mama's overall comfort demanded the effort. The more Mama had bowel problems, the more time she was likely to spend soiled, and the more frequently she would have to endure being cleaned, or scrubbed, which contributed further to the irritation of her already fragile skin. The nursing home staff insisted that they gave their residents individual attention, but in practice, the regimentation of the institution perpetually won out. The only conditions that got dietary consideration were those that were medically sanctioned as affecting significant numbers of residents. A whole block of people who were diabetic or required a salt-restricted diet could be handled, but leaving chocolate off someone's tray was outside their scope.

Another concept that flummoxed the nursing home was the idea that a resident might not need to eat three full meals a day. In general, disabled nursing home residents, like children, are typically pressured to eat all that they are served. For elders with digestive problems, this practice succeeds only in overloading and aggravating their already distressed digestive systems. Forcing the consumption of food is as much a social convention as it is an attempt to maintain a resident's weight—although the latter has become a significant driving force because of historical abuses in the nursing home industry. Not so many years ago, nursing home operators were fattening their purses by failing to provide enough food for their hapless charges. Once this came to light, the starving of old people naturally offended the public and led to the implementation of caloric requirements for all nursing home residents. The weights of residents are

monitored through monthly weigh-ins, dutifully recorded in charts that are periodically examined by official
inspectors. It is unquestionably necessary that people
who must rely on others to furnish them with food
should be provided with enough adequate nutrition to
maintain good health and appropriate body weight.
However, in solving this problem, another one was
created.

I watched Mama become increasingly unable to
tolerate physically the amount of food she was given.
Now that she no longer had the power to self-regulate,
she agreeably let the people who fed her spoon it in for
as long as they liked. After months of struggling with
the nursing home, I finally succeeded in getting the
requirement for how much Mama was expected to consume per meal reduced from 100 percent to 70 percent.
However, since the same amount of food was still served
and the recorded requirement often went unnoticed, this
in no way kept the aides from feeding her all the food
anyway, and they continued to cheerfully report to me
that "she ate 100 percent."

In the aftermath of my mother's stroke, I learned
that assistive feeding and forced feeding are two different things, though the line between the two can become
obscured. Assistive feeding, which is what Mama
required, is a sound policy in which someone who is
willing and able to eat but who simply cannot feed herself or eat in the usual manner is fed. Withholding food
from such a person would be, in effect, a form of
euthanasia. However, typical nursing home policy on
feeding dependent residents often goes beyond being

merely assistive, resulting in what amounts to being force fed. In Mama's case, a more personally suited approach to feeding her would not only have decreased her difficulties but might also have enabled her to thrive for a while. Often, people who are approaching death no longer wish to eat or are gradually unable to comfortably consume enough food to maintain themselves; to force them to eat or to make them eat more than their bodies can handle seems indecent and even abusive.

When Mama was fed in the dining room, she was wheeled back to her room afterward and left to sit unattended until an aide came in to perform whatever was next in Mama's schedule. Since many of the aides and nurses took their meal breaks after the patients' meal times, and the few left on duty were busy tending other residents, the hallways and nurses station were virtually deserted for the hour following meals. I truly was afraid that with Mama being left alone after she had been fed, she might begin to choke, and no one would be there to help her. I literally begged the nursing staff to watch her closely after meals. They insisted that they were paying attention, but how could they be if no one was around or within earshot?

Mama usually seemed to be doing fine during her meals, so there were no signals to indicate that she needed to be fed less food more slowly. Ten minutes to a half an hour later, when the aide who had fed her was long gone, the trouble would start. Accompanied by dramatic guttural noises and unseemly gestures as well as obvious discomfort, Mama would begin to part company with the recently consumed meal, and at the same time, she would develop a lot of mucous and respiratory difficulty. These episodes were disquieting, to say the least. With coaxing she could sometimes spit out the mucous, but mostly it just stayed in her throat.

The eventual medical response to Mama's recurring post-meal congestion was to wheel a machine into her room that suctioned the mucous from her throat. Although it was an invasive procedure, it was at least quick and effective, and Mama endured it stoically. I was frustrated by the mentality behind all this, however, that allowed a situation to escalate to the point of requiring intrusive and uncomfortable interventions when no effort was being made to prevent the problem in the first place. My only consolation was that at least they were doing *something* to alleviate Mama's difficulties.

Additionally, Mama was prescribed daily respiratory treatments to be given to her by the nurses. This involved placing over Mama's nose and mouth a mask that emitted medicated vapor, which would help to clear her congestion. The treatments seemed to help, but between the nurses not having time to give them because of their busy schedules and Mama often removing the mask if she was awake and unattended, she didn't always get the full benefit. Once I walked into Mama's room when she was having one of these treatments. "Whatcha doin', Mama?" I asked casually. She looked at me for a moment and in a low voice, saturated with boredom— or perhaps it was disgust, I wasn't sure—she replied, "Breathing . . ."

As any body moves toward that inexorable final event of death, the functionality of one organ system after another begins to degenerate. Appetite begins to decline, along with the ability to absorb nutrients, and weight loss is the natural outcome. Since nursing home residents are seldom considered to be officially dying until they are almost gasping their last breaths, the shutting-down process is ruthlessly impeded when food is scooped, even squirted, into bodies that no longer have the wherewithal to resist and that must then struggle to continue digesting the food.

Throughout her stay in the nursing home, Mama continued to experience sporadic spells of internal bleeding. Dr. Klink advised me that a colonoscopy should be performed on my mother. This would entail a trip to the hospital where a tube would be inserted through her rectum and into her large intestine so that doctors could take a look at what was happening. While I am sure it is a great medical advance, I did not have the slightest intention of letting my mother be put through such an undignified and intrusive procedure. The doctor argued with me vigorously. At the same time, he admitted that if the procedure did reveal something, she was not strong enough to endure drug therapy, let alone surgery. The doctor seemed unable to relinquish the importance of a diagnosis; in fact, he proceeded to give Mama the examination against my wishes. It was Dr. Klink's last act as Mama's physician, unless you count the long letter he wrote to me accusing me of not caring about my mother. The results of the colonoscopy? She was suffering from bleeding diverticuli, for which surgery to remove the offending tissue was ill-advised given her condition. Had she continued to bleed, it would have been a pretty gentle way for her to go, but she wasn't that lucky. With each episode, the bleeding stopped spontaneously.

The diagnosis brought into focus the connection between rectal bleeding and Mama's intestinal ailments, providing yet another consequence of the continued, inconsiderate feeding practices. Individualized treatment plans are effectively blocked when regulations are divorced from the necessary flexibility to respond to real people's changing daily needs. Such policies make it nearly impossible to distinguish between elders who can flourish for a time if their life force is given more appropriate support and encouragement, and elders who are irrevocably moving through the last stages of physical disintegration. The needs of neither group are met, the former needing care that will enhance their health, and the latter needing recognition and support for their journey into death. Instead, many elders get driven toward death in a senseless and unnecessarily uncomfortable manner.

Emotional involvement can distort even the most informed family members' perspectives enough to make it very difficult to ascertain what course of care is appropriate. It should be the responsibility of the physicians to determine when a person has entered a terminal phase and then to tailor the treatment plan accordingly. The hospice movement has made great strides in providing care-plan guidance for people who are dying of specific terminal illnesses, but the recommendations often do not apply to the way people die in nursing homes. In addition, the active presence of hospice in long term care facilities is still relatively rare, partly because only private pay patients are generally eligible for the Medicare hospice benefit, which excludes all the dying elders who are dependent on Medicaid.

An evaluation system specially designed for the very old is needed. With this system must come closely scrutinized safeguards to ensure that residents are not deemed terminal when all that is driving them downhill is the abysmal treatment they are receiving. Getting hospice more involved is important in finding a solution to appropriate end-of-life care. Just recently the National Hospice and Palliative Care Organization (formerly the National Hospice Organization) has expanded its scope to include nonterminal palliative care, focusing on easing suffering rather than curing disease. This could mean reduced suffering for millions of people who are not yet in an officially terminal state. An even more critical need is training for nursing home staff to enable them to understand what palliative care is and to identify when to apply it. A philosophical shift throughout the nursing home industry, and indeed throughout society, is critical for implementing such a change.

These insights have come to me after the fact. When I was "in the trenches," I didn't really think beyond the constant struggle of getting Mama adequate daily treatment. It never took me long during any visit to generate a list of notes and issues to go over with the various people overseeing Mama's care. The doctor, administrator, nurses, social workers, and anyone else I thought could make a difference were liable to hear from me, in person while I was there or via long-distance telephone calls after I returned home. I made strenuous efforts to approach all of them with diplomacy and empathy, asking them for their perspective on whatever had upset me. As a result, I usually found a sympathetic ear and received promises to do better.

From my own experiences working in nursing homes, I knew what the staff were up against. I also knew the difference between conscientious, caring workers laboring under trying circumstances and workers who were just doing time and collecting a paycheck. I had no sympathy for the latter and was frustrated each time I saw such workers still at their jobs. The support I received came from the supervising nurses, some of whom were clearly dedicated and committed to a high standard of service. Unfortunately, they usually lacked the means to bring about its delivery, including the time to observe care firsthand.

It seems that, as a society, there is too much willingness to shrug our shoulders and say, well, that's just how nursing homes are. The disturbing events that take place in nursing homes are not a rallying point for a widely embraced social cause, even though most people have a negative image of these institutions. In addition, many of those who promote and profit from nursing homes resist efforts to improve the quality of residents' lives and the working conditions of the staff. I have spoken to scores of people who readily share grim stories about nursing homes where someone they know has resided. Some people dismiss this crisis in our society by resolving never to go to a nursing home. But they don't realize that in reality, many people wind up needing the kind of care presently available only in an institutional setting—and when they find themselves in need of that care, they discover that they don't have much say about, or control over, its quality.

It seems ironic that we live in a time in which we have the capacity to live longer than we ever have before, yet so many people dread the thought of living too long because they fear they will have only misery to look forward to. Imagine what it would feel like if we could anticipate old age as a time to retire in the best sense of the word, if it were a time we could anticipate with confidence. What if we knew that when we needed it, we would receive compassionate, high-quality care as we made the inevitable journey into physical decline? What if we could count on knowing that we would be surrounded by people who were sensitive to what we were going through, and who regarded us as valuable human beings no matter how little we could participate in the world around us?

As a society, we tend to reject the aged because we fear what we see. But aging into physical decline and increased dependence is as much a part of the natural life cycle as being born helpless and growing gradually more independent. In truth, if we live long enough, we leave this world much as we entered it. Wouldn't it show true wisdom to treat the last stage of life with the same tenderness and concern as we do infancy? We have not yet come to terms with how necessary it is to provide for people who not only took care of themselves but, in many cases, once took care of us as well. Despite wanting desperately to help these people, their burgeoning needs can sometimes seem a nuisance or burden. If certain systems were put in place that would allow the aged and the ill to be understood and to have their needs properly addressed, the burden would be eased immensely.

Forecasts predict that more than one half of all elderly women and one third of all elderly men will reside in a nursing home before they die. Within our reach, and in some areas already being implemented, are ways to reduce these ratios. Through means such as improved education about geriatric health care, outreach programs including home health care that enable elders to stay at home longer, and widespread availability of intermediary foster care homes for those who require assistance with the activities of daily living, we can go a long way toward reducing the number of elderly people needing nursing homes. (It is important to note, too, that today's assisted living facilities, despite their homelike settings, often suffer from the same shortcomings as skilled nursing facilities. Too many of them are no more than physical custodians, short-changing the psychological and social needs of their wards.) Even with the improvements in geriatric care, the foreseeable future will continue to find many elderly and other disabled citizens requiring the level of services presently offered only in long term, skilled nursing facilities such as nursing homes.

We are approaching a time in the very near future when for the first time in history the majority of the population will be senior citizens. This situation will demand that we relate very differently to the final stage of life than we did in the twentieth century. As we all are aging, we should expect to be treated with the same consideration and thoroughness at old age as at any other stage of life. I believe the day will come when it will no longer be acceptable to respond to the problems facing an elderly person by saying, "Well, you're old. What can you expect?" and believe it to be a rhetorical question.

15

SLIPPING AWAY

With what strife and pains we come into the world
we know not, but 'tis commonly no easy matter to
get out of it.
Thomas Browne

I FIND IT DIFFICULT to convey what it felt like
to live with a constant sense of dread and emergency,
to have my heart leap into my throat every time the
telephone rang, wondering—*What now?* Knowing that
much of what Mama suffered in the nursing home was
needless and that the family's constant attention was
required just to keep things from getting worse added
immensely to the distress of seeing her endure such difficult and limiting circumstances. I am convinced that
despite her age and deteriorating condition, my mother
would not have experienced nearly the number of ailments that she did, had the overall quality of her care
been better.

Since we never knew what we would find when we
walked into Mama's room at the nursing home, apprehension followed us like a dark cloud, especially since we

so often found Mama in some poor state. For me, whether I was dealing with a crisis, trying to get Mama cleaned up after an "accident," or searching for lost laundry, it always felt as though I were swimming with all my might toward an ever-receding shore. Unmitigated vigilance was demanded, but I had to pick my battles wisely since there was no way I could fight them all. I knew that even if things seemed okay at some juncture, I could never take Mama's care for granted. What a luxury it would have been simply to focus all my attention on being with her and supporting her through that time in her life, feeling confident that those being paid to see to her daily care were doing so in an efficient, effective, and compassionate manner.

Even when the hours at Mama's bedside wore long on the days when she couldn't seem to open her eyes to the outside world, I was always aware of the preciousness of the time we still had together. I relished the intimacy of quietly watching her sleep, of noting the many details of her skin, her hair, the shape of her hands, her face. She always looked beautiful to me. Her body was so aged, but it had all the uniqueness and character that only something very worn can have. I felt awe as I gazed at her and considered that I had come from her.

The degree of my involvement, combined with the effort of addressing the lapses in Mama's care, made it no easy matter to keep myself up and running. It was not unusual for me to suffer from one physical ailment or another after I spent time at the nursing home. So I learned to take breaks when I needed them, to go do a little shopping or get something to eat. Finding a balance—and not letting myself feel as though I were betraying my mother for taking time out for myself—helped me to find the strength to cope with the nursing home. I needed to be at my best during the time that I spent with her.

My brothers visited Mama when they could but did not share my background in dealing with details of her care. I was thankful that one of them handled all the paperwork, sparing me from laboring over the bills. My sister, while very supportive of me, was dealing with the death of her husband and did not directly involve herself with the nursing home. Aunt Margaret continued to visit Mama nearly every day, kept away only by icy roads and occasional bouts with her own ill health. It was an incredible comfort to know that Mama had the consistent presence of a family member throughout her stay. Some of my cousins also visited Mama, and I was grateful that they came, providing thoughtful relief to the monotony of Mama's days. One cousin in particular was great at teasing Mama and making her laugh.

It was naturally difficult to oversee Mama's care from such a long distance. Although Aunt Margaret was devoted to her sister, being in her late seventies and in failing health herself made the stress of dealing with the nursing home extra hard on her. I depended on her, though, to alert me to any changes in Mama's condition, and she depended on me to handle most of the confrontations. Even though the nursing staff were supposed to inform me of changes with Mama, it was often the other way around.

I've never held much faith in the saying "An old

dog can't learn new tricks." Aunt Margaret seemed to grow a lot during this time, thanks to her being open minded enough to try new approaches. I suggested ways of acting and of phrasing things so she could be more effectively assertive, which enabled her to feel more empowered and therefore more willing to address problems that required immediate attention. She learned to balance her resentment toward staff negligence by noticing and acknowledging the times when they did do a good job at something.

I designed some charts regarding aspects of Mama's care for Aunt Margaret to fill out every day. They provided her with a simple medium for recording the conditions she found and were a concise way to pass the information on to me. They also gave her a means to relieve some of the distress and frustration I knew she felt when she found Mama's care lacking in some way. I hoped that once I accumulated a few weeks' worth of these documents, they would remove some of the perceived subjectivity of Mama's situation and provide something more concrete to work with.

I believe the charts are a good idea that can work well for some families, but for us they proved to be too little too late. They were not as easy for my aging aunt to use as I had hoped, although they did provide me with a clearer picture of what aspects of Mama's care were occasionally versus routinely neglected. Unfortunately, the nursing home personnel tended to be persistently defensive despite my efforts to maintain a diplomatic and cooperative, if relentless, approach with them. They compensated for their lapses in care with a tendency to blame the family, as though our complaints rather than their carelessness were the actual problem.

It hurt me deeply to find wet, cold vomit that no one had cleaned up soaked through Mama's clothes, or to find her lying in her long-cold incontinence. I ached at the thought of Mama sitting or lying there, staring, waiting, not knowing how much time would pass before someone arrived to help her. The repeated insults to Mama's dignity were devastating, eroding my peace of mind. How could I not request that someone tend to her without delay? I would do what I could myself until help arrived, but for the rest of the time we would just have to sit together and wait.

It wasn't Mama's helplessness to care for herself that bothered me so much. This was one of those things in life that nothing can be done about, so I chose not to agonize over it. Often when I assisted in her care, it would occur to me how many times she had undoubtedly cared for me in similar fashion. It seemed as though we had come full circle from the beginning of my life to the end of hers. What bothered me so much was that unlike the devoted care she had provided for me as a child, the treatment she was receiving now was neither doting nor timely.

Seeing loved ones suffer is always painful. Knowing they are suffering unnecessarily is all but unbearable. While family members are in the midst of the emotional intensity of having a loved one in a nursing home, it can be difficult to know what is and what is not avoidable suffering. It is the nature of life that illness and time eventually ravage a body and wear it out. I struggled time and again to ascertain what was inevitable and what was preventable, and therefore what I should accept as part and parcel of Mama's condition and what I should make an issue of. I easily became misled by medical personnel who were not inclined to pursue certain matters. The more they tried to placate me, rather than admit to problems or offer solutions, the more uneasy I felt.

In addition to what I could learn over the phone from Aunt Margaret and various nursing home personnel, I tried as best I could to monitor Mama through direct contact with her. I telephoned her at least once a week. Consideration for the staff kept me from calling more often, since each connection meant calling the nurses station first and imposing on someone to go answer Mama's telephone and then hold it to her ear while we talked.

When I spoke with Mama on the phone, I always asked her how she was. Most of the time she would answer, "I'm all right." I knew this was her way to let me know that she was hanging in there, that I shouldn't worry, and that things were pretty normal, as poor as "normal" was. It is amazing how much can be conveyed by so few words when the person speaking to you is so familiar. Every once in a while she mentioned a pain somewhere or that she didn't feel well, which I always followed up on with the nurse on duty. Beyond that, our conversations didn't amount to much in terms of content, but being able to say that we loved each other felt very important. Hard to bear were the days when she was too sleepy or when her speech was too garbled for me to understand her, but I learned to accept those days as just the way it was sometimes.

We had been enjoying a long period of particularly lucid and connected phone calls up until the last two months of Mama's life when she began to have increased difficulty communicating. Little conversation took place between us, and when Mama did speak, I often couldn't understand what she was saying. She would also fall asleep a lot. But somehow, one thing continued to come across more clearly and emphatically than ever. She would say to me, "I love you, darling, very much." I do not know what it took for her to pull that statement together when everything else she said was virtually unintelligible, but I appreciated it deeply.

In hindsight, I realize it was evident that Mama's condition was deteriorating those last few months, but I did not see it at the time nor did the nursing home staff say anything. A few months earlier we had been advised that Mama's G-tube needed to be replaced, but within weeks of its replacement, the area around the opening had become irritated and raw. I was repeatedly assured that all efforts were being made to treat the excoriation, but the area remained red, raw, and oozing as though this violation of Mama's abdomen was erupting in anger. There seemed to be considerable disagreement among the various nurses as to what sort of treatment was most appropriate. Some insisted on bandaging the area, while others felt certain that air was necessary and removed the bandage. Frustrated, I contacted Dr. Hyde, who then issued orders that at least provided a consistent approach to treatment.

In addition, food had begun to seep out from around the tube after meals, as though Mama's body was determined to no longer absorb the meals that were being spooned into it. Unable to ameliorate these problems, the unit nurse advised me that she would like to remove the G-tube. She asserted that it wasn't worth the trouble it was causing, especially since it was seldom used anymore. She mentioned that several of the residents had recently had their G-tubes removed and that the openings in their stomachs had healed cleanly and promptly.

The removal of the G-tube was a momentous decision since there was no way the surgery could ever be repeated. Goodness knows I had certainly never felt comfortable knowing there was a hole in my mother's stomach. The way the staff poured things in there as though she were an inanimate object had always made me cringe. Removing the tube felt like an opportunity to restore Mama in some small way. However, I was not willing to grant permission for the removal based on my feelings alone. So I consulted Dr. Hyde, who did not hesitate to give his endorsement.

It had been over two and a half years since Mama's stroke. I felt battered by all that I had witnessed and had dealt with in that time, as though I were at the bottom of an avalanche and more snow just kept piling up. I have become aware in retrospect that Mama suffered frequently, maybe even continuously, from some degree of dehydration. To make matters worse, her dehydration came to the attention of Mama's caregivers only when it reached the point of displaying significant clinical symptoms. This is an example of an ineffective medical approach that frequently fails to maintain health and is geared instead to respond only after health has failed.

I relayed my concern about Mama getting adequate fluids without the G-tube, knowing that she was seldom able to consume enough during meals. The unit nurse acknowledged the need for liquids and promised me that she would see to it that each shift gave Mama something to drink. I worried about that. Giving Mama liquids through the tube was something a nurse could do quickly and without assistance from Mama. Giving Mama anything orally was another matter since it required that she not only be awake (which she often wasn't by that time, nor could she be readily roused) but also that someone take the time to let her sip gradually rather than pour it all in at once. Knowing that both time and the patience that might accompany it are nearly always in short supply in nursing homes, I anticipated eventual problems.

"Eventually" came less than a week after the removal of the G-tube. A very distressed Aunt Margaret called me from the nursing home to report that Mama was very weak, could not be roused, and had not eaten since the previous day. The usual flurry of phone calls on my part quickly netted me enough information to conclude that Mama was probably dehydrated. I suggested this to the nurse on duty that evening, and she agreed that it made sense. She told me that she was unaware that during her shift Mama was supposed to be given fluids. When I spoke with yet another nurse on a day shift the following afternoon, she told me she also was

unaware that she should be giving Mama fluids between
meals. She looked in the chart while I was on the line
and stated emphatically that there was no such order.
When I brought this to the attention of the unit nurse,
I was met with a wall of denial. Dr. Hyde was no help,
either, and I began to think that, gerontologist or not, he
wasn't a doctor I could count on.

Mama was put on intravenous fluids and in a couple of days she seemed to rally. I clung helplessly to the
hope that after this incident more attention would be
paid to her need for fluids. Knowing that it was one
more thing I needed to monitor, I called more frequently than usual to inquire about Mama's condition. In retrospect I realize they had provided me with false assurances more than actual information. Aunt Margaret has
since told me that she felt the same way. Even though
she was there nearly every day, she didn't always know
how to interpret what she saw.

On the Sunday following Thanksgiving, not long
before Mama's final crisis, Aunt Margaret arrived for a
visit and walked in on a wrenching scene. The young
male aide who had ignored Mama's friendly greeting
several months earlier was feeding Mama with his back
turned to her while watching a football game on her TV.
Both she and her bed clothes were spattered with food.
To feed someone without even looking or making
human contact is deplorable. And being at the high risk
for aspiration that Mama was, it was exceedingly dangerous, too. Our outraged complaints were met with
more hollow apologies—and the young man continued
his employment at the nursing home.

I have come to suspect that the nursing home staff had become increasingly overwhelmed with caring for a person who needed as much care and attention as my mother. The more disabled a resident is, the more time-consuming is their care. I am haunted by the thought that the staff had grown weary of bothering with my mother and began systematically, if not consciously, to neglect her even more. Maybe it is foolish of me to torment myself with such thoughts. Certainly what happened to Mama is not unique; it is happening to elders in nursing homes all over this country every day.

I will always feel sorrow for what my dear mother had to live through in that nursing home. It isn't that I can't accept the fact that she had to live out her last days in an institution. Even if our family had been affluent enough to provide round-the-clock care for her in a home setting, I am not sure that would have been the best possible solution. A high-quality, group setting could have been ideal, with its greater opportunities for fellowship and stimulation. It was not Mama's helplessness or her time-ravaged body that was so painful to see, either. It was the parade of aides and nurses who treated her with callous disregard, and it was the nursing home establishment itself, which failed to maintain standards of care that I know are achievable.

I find grace in the fact that the sorrow is always accompanied by sweet memories of Mama's smile, her loving eyes, and her voice telling me that she loves me. Her soft, wavy hair, with its few stubbornly persistent strands of auburn, was gorgeous to the end. Her pretty, light-green eyes, which gradually turned bluish and then gray, along with her pale, rose-tinged skin, were offset just right by her white hair. The changes that illness and age had wrought were like the crinkles and cracks of an old photograph. You could see the wear and tear, but it didn't disguise the unfailing beauty for one moment.

16

THE FULL MOON SETS

And when the earth shall claim your limbs, then
shall you truly dance.

Kahlil Gibran, The Prophet

A LATE SUMMER VISIT with Mama had ended on
an especially sweet note. Even though all the usual hustle and bustle was going on around us, it seemed as
though we were enveloped more than ever in our own
private world. I remember how quiet she was, how tran-
quil it felt to sit with her, just being ourselves there
together. Sometimes we gazed into one another's eyes
for long periods of time. She seemed peaceful, not agitated at all. Although Mama slept a lot during that visit,
whenever she awoke, she seemed quietly alert. I fussed
over her some, as I tended to do, but her calm demeanor
had a soothing effect on me.

I was preparing to leave, but I wanted to get her
through lunch first. I always liked to know everything
was running smoothly, at least for the moment, before I
walked out the door. I was feeling fluttery, anxious, the

way I did when I knew I would soon have to part from
her. She wasn't the least bit interested in the lunch the
aide brought her, which flustered me a little since feeding Mama was one of the few things I could do for her.

I was so distracted by my efforts to get Mama
started on lunch that it took some time before I noticed
how intently she was watching me and following every
move that I made. It was the look on her face that
stopped me. Her eyes were glowing, brimming with the
most tender, adoring love imaginable. I gazed back in
silence, immersed in this wonderfully fulfilling moment.
Nothing else mattered, not the stroke, not the nursing
home—it was just us, full and at peace. I remember the
scene so vividly because it was the last time my mother
ever looked at me.

The day the nurse called me with the news of what
would be Mama's last trauma had been an oddly empty
sort of day for me. Although I had been recuperating for
several weeks from a car accident, on this particular day
it seemed as though I had been sidelined since mid-
morning for no apparent reason. I was not ill or in pain,
nor was I particularly tired; I simply had no urge to do
anything. I literally laid in bed all day, not sleeping
much, not even reading. I just lay there quietly, resting,
letting time pass. It was just getting dark, a little after
five o'clock, when the phone rang. When I answered it,
I recognized the voice of the nurse whose kindness I had
come to appreciate the past few weeks. She informed me
that Mama had aspirated a short while after dinner and
was not expected to live through the night. The senseless
calamity I had long feared was coming to pass.

Images played through my mind. I knew Mama had most likely been left alone after a meal and had regurgitated and wound up with something going down the wrong pipe and into her lungs. I wondered whether the staff had put her to bed too soon or had forgotten to elevate her head. I felt too vulnerable over the telephone to ask right then, doubting that my questions would be answered truthfully anyway. What happened had happened, and dealing with it was all I could do. I was frightened and distraught, struggling to maintain control over both my voice and my thoughts. I wanted to be able to comprehend what I would need to do next. I knew for sure that this time there would be no hesitating. Despite the previous crises in which dire predictions had not materialized, I knew this time it was really happening.

I asked the nurse to tell me how the nursing home intended to proceed. Once she finished, I hung up and called an emergency room nurse at the hospital closest to the nursing home, who convinced me that nothing could be done at the hospital that couldn't be done at the nursing home. I was thankful that at least Mama wouldn't need to be moved. A few frantic hours followed as I called numerous airlines, finally finding a flight out at 11 P.M. I began to pack furiously and called some friends to find someone to look after my cat while I was gone. No one was home (there's some law about that, right?), so I left many messages. At last someone called back, and we made arrangements.

As I packed, I tried to figure out what to take. What did I need to read, for myself and to Mama? What were the right words to have with me for my mother's death? I had been reading a book about dying that described many rituals that are supposed to be necessary for the proper passage from life into death. Should I bring it with me? What should I do? The answer came loud and clear from within me. I already had what I needed. No props, no guide books, I just needed to go and be with Mama. I made one more phone call to check on Mama's condition, and then I was in my car, alone in the night, rushing toward the airport.

I felt surprisingly calm as I drove down the dark highway toward Albuquerque. In spite of the urgency, I was careful not to throw myself off balance by becoming frantic. Once at the airport, I parked, checked my bags, and entered my boarding gate's waiting area. I was very alert, very contained. With few flights available on such short notice, I had to settle for traveling by way of Las Vegas. It was frustrating to head west before I could go east to where Mama was. But I reminded myself that sometimes in order to get where we are going, we must first do something that may seem to lead us away from our goal.

The Las Vegas airport was buzzing at midnight with as much activity as most terminals have at noon. Truly this seemed a place that never sleeps. I was emptied from the gate into a large, brightly lit room, at the center of which were numerous slot machines, arranged like some strange metal and plastic twentieth-century Stonehenge. By then I was starving, not having eaten since early in the day. I hesitated, though; it didn't seem right to eat at such a time, but hunger pangs made me acknowledge that I was living—and required food. I thought of how my mother and father had always devoted themselves to keeping me fed, and how they had worried about me not eating enough once they realized what a finicky, light eater I was. I made a silent promise to them that I would not neglect to feed myself. The fast-food vegetarian burrito tasted delicious and made me feel nurtured and grounded. I called the nursing home again to check on Mama's condition. I learned that my friend Sandy had arrived and was sitting with Aunt Margaret beside Mama's bed. Knowing they were there and that they were praying for Mama provided an anchor. They were holding the space for me, and Mama was waiting.

The plane ride out of Las Vegas was blessedly dark, and I had a row of seats to myself. I thought about the two tall angels I had seen so many times in my mind's eye at the head of Mama's bed and began to actively visualize them. Jesus was there, too, holding his hand over Mama's heart. This had become a vivid and familiar scene. I remembered that the book I had left at home told of the importance of visualizing something like that for a dying person. I applied myself to it but immediately felt the artificiality of what I was doing. I realized that neither the angels nor Jesus required me to sustain their presence. They were simply there, and I was blessed with the recognition of it. I let my mind rest, let myself be comforted by the understanding that Mama was in the hands of Love, and that it wasn't all up to me. Sweet grace.

I noticed a TV monitor above the seat in front of

me and saw someone singing. I hadn't asked the airline attendant for headphones, but I could still faintly hear enough to know that the performer was singing "My Favorite Things." This started me thinking about all of Mama's favorite things. There were so many beautiful, inspiring, and pleasant things she loved. I began to name them to myself, intent on remembering everything: hummingbirds; lilacs; trees; lemon meringue pie; autumn; the color green; "Greensleeves"; songs from *My Fair Lady* and *Dr. Zhivago*; the poems of James Whitcomb Riley; early American decor; ducks, both live and decoy; bananas; grandly appointed old homes; San Francisco; cruise ships; the ocean; sunsets; walking in the rain; her family; her children . . . me.

I stayed awake the whole trip, waiting in the dark, loving Mama with all my heart, calling out to her that I was coming. Finally, the plane landed in Indianapolis. With heart pounding, I proceeded to collect my bags from the overhead compartment and then sought out my rental car. I considered calling the nursing home but decided against it. If Mama had gone on, I didn't want to hear about it in the airport with a half-hour drive still ahead of me. I drove to the nursing home in the pre-dawn, fast but cautiously. Each moment was so acute, so noticed. Driving into the nursing home parking lot, I took each long step across the pavement, into the building, down the hallway, focused only on my destination. Down the first corridor, left and down the middle corridor, no one around to get in my way, left at the nurses station, not looking at them, not wanting any news. Nothing mattered but my reaching Mama's bedside.

When I entered the room, I saw at once that Mama had indeed waited for me to come. Despite the circumstances, I was unfailingly glad to be with Mama again, touching her, stroking her, pouring my love out to her and into her. Her breathing was labored, and her left eye was part-way open. I reassured her that I had come and would be by her side. Within a few minutes her breathing eased, and soon her eye shut. I felt her resting, and something eased within me, too. We were together now. We could do this.

The vigil continued as I sat with Mama all day, waiting, watching for some sign, some change. I clung to the hope that she might wake up once more, but I knew that I didn't need her to. We could have looked into one another's eyes and said "I love you" a thousand more times, but we didn't *need* to. It eased my heart to see her resting peacefully. Although her breathing was taking great effort as her chest heaved and her open mouth sucked in air, she didn't appear to be struggling otherwise. Periodically I dozed, resting my head on the edge of the bed, next to Mama's side.

The immediate crisis of the aspiration had passed, but it all had obviously greatly weakened Mama. The nursing home staff had given her morphine to ease the discomfort of the aspiration. This surprised me since the nurse I had spoken with at the hospital had told me that a patient in Mama's condition would never be given morphine due to the danger of it excessively depressing her respiration. I was told by the nursing home staff that it was unlikely that Mama would survive much longer, that she was actually in a coma, and that it was only a matter of time now—hours, days, even weeks, no one could say.

I had been afraid all day to leave Mama's side, reluctant even to go to the bathroom, lest she slip away while I wasn't there. But as the shadows of the night engulfed the room, I remembered the arduous lesson I had learned about taking care of myself. It had been thirty-six hours since I last had slept, and I was at the point of exhaustion where I would no longer be able to function. Sitting there in a chair next to the bed for days on end was not going to work; I was going to have to lie down and sleep, at least for a little while. I whispered into Mama's ear, reminding her that I was with her, that everything was okay, that she should just rest now, and that I needed to go rest now, too. Assured that she was as comfortable as she could be, and with promises from the nurses to call me immediately if there was any change, I drove the few miles to Aunt Margaret's home. After a shower and some food, I went to sleep immediately, feeling a strong sense that it would be okay— Mama wouldn't die before I returned.

Well before dawn I awoke and quickly prepared to return to the nursing home. Everything had an intense vividness as I drove toward the nursing home, gliding through the dark, deserted streets in the frosty December air. I barely dared to breathe in the enormity of what was happening. As I whisked along Main Street toward my turn, my heart quickened at a beautiful sight. A pale-orange full moon glowed majestically, solemnly, and oh, so silently through the bare branches of a grove of trees to the west. The moon was setting. (Months later I had a dream where I was watching just such a moonset with Mama. "There she goes . . . ," I heard her say.)

Once more I found myself pulling into the parking lot of the nursing home. I took a moment before I entered the building to drink in the bracing outdoor air. As always, I walked briskly through the corridors, intent only on my destination. I swept into Mama's room, calling to her, "I'm back, Mama. I'm back."

There hadn't been any changes since I had left the night before. A nurse informed me that Mama hadn't passed any urine for more than twenty-four hours in spite of the IV fluids I had requested she be given to avoid dehydration. I hated the thought of Mama being thirsty. I remembered how she once told me that *she* couldn't stand the thought of someone being thirsty because of not being able to ask for a drink. She had always made sure to offer water frequently to us children when we were too young to ask.

It was hard to accept that Mama was dying, so I concentrated on learning what was happening in the moment. I wanted someone to tell me what was going on and what to expect. I was glad when the nurse from Dr. Hyde's office came to examine Mama. She told me straight out that it was likely Mama's kidneys were shutting down (which I knew was a sign of the death process), and that the end was near. The IV wouldn't help and would only prolong the inevitable. She convinced me that Mama was not experiencing thirst or discomfort, so I let them remove it. It was a wrenching feeling, but at that point there was no question of holding on. I asked for one of the flavored little dental swabs. I dipped it into some water and used it to moisten Mama's lips and tongue. Her mouth closed around the sponge, sucking out the drops of moisture. I anguished at the thought that she was indeed experiencing thirst but hoped fervently that it was just a reflex.

I resisted my urge to fuss over her further, knowing it was time just to let her be, to let her rest. The nurses came in frequently to minister to her in various ways, taking blood pressure and other readings. I was grateful when they finally stopped coming and we were left alone. Revived after my night's rest, I settled in by Mama's side.

I said all the things to her that I had always hoped I would when the time came. I let her know how much she was loved, how her life had been just the way it was supposed to be, how there was nothing she should regret. I told her she was beautiful and perfect exactly the way she was. I assured her that she was not simply that body, and there was no need to hold onto it. I even joked about how she never liked to waste anything and wouldn't throw out anything until it was completely used up. I told her I thought she had gotten all the use out of her body that a person possibly could have. So just let it go, I told her, just slip out of that body, out of suffering and into freedom. I told her what I know to be true with all my heart—"You are radiance and love. You have always been radiance and love."

The phone rang, and it was Sandy. As soon as I answered, Mama took a very big, raucous breath.

"Mama?!" I quickly hung up the phone and clasped Mama's hand as I called out to her again. There was a long pause without breath, and then she took another long, gasping one. I knew that death was present. For a second, panic welled up in me, and I extended my arm toward the call button. "No," I told myself. "We can do this."

"It's all right, Mama," I told her, calming myself at the same time. "It's all right." Another long breathless pause, another deep breath, and then silence. I waited. Infinitely long seconds. No more breaths. No more heartbeat. No more suffering for this beloved Mother. It was over, and she was free. I knew that the angels had her. Waves of exhilarating joy filled my heart. "You're free, Mama. You're free!" My heart blew prayers into the wings of the angels.

Once I was sure that all was well and was finished, I succumbed to my grief. I laid my head down on Mama's now silent chest and sobbed my love for this body and this being. Time passed, in wonder, joy, and awesome sorrow.

At three o'clock a nurse came in to tell me I had a phone call out at the desk. With the stubbornness of a child who is unsure of her rights but certain of her will, I told the nurse I wasn't going out there. Mama had passed on, and I was not leaving her. Without remark, she turned and left, but she returned a moment later with a stethoscope. I watched silently as she enacted the necessary death ritual. The phone call the nurse had told me about was routed to Mama's room and when I answered it, my nephew Andy was on the line. I was grateful for his voice, his presence, and later for his comfort in the raw days to come.

I continued to sit with Mama, aware of a sense of simultaneous holiness and ordinariness. I alternated between venting my grief and soberly attending to the business of Mama's death. As I had tried to protect her in life, I continued to do so in death. I was determined that she be left undisturbed for a while, feeling that it was reverent. And, to be honest, I wanted some time to say good-bye before her body was removed from my sight forever.

Finally, as evening shadows filled the room once again, I let the aides prepare her body. Together we bathed and dressed her one last time. My stomach knotted as I saw two big, bloody bed sores exposed when they turned her over. I noticed an aide weeping as she thoughtfully fastened a little, gold, guardian angel pin to Mama's robe. The men from the mortuary arrived soon after. Being well practiced in the art of treading lightly at such moments, they stepped back and allowed me to say good-bye once more. I placed one last tender kiss on Mama's cool cheek and watched numbly as they covered her body and took it away. Left alone in the room, I cleared her night stand of any evidence of illness, leaving only the flowers and candle I had bought earlier, when I had stepped out to let Aunt Margaret say her good-byes to Mama. I stared at the empty bed and smoothed the sheets, honoring this place of my mother's passing.

I lay awake in the dark that night, immersed in its depths. I felt bereft, lost at the thought of being in a world without my mother. . . . And then she was there, embracing me with her unfettered love, and I knew she had not left me and never would. She gently covered me in a blanket of comfort, and I smiled and closed my eyes.

17

PUSHING, PULLING, AND JUST STANDING STILL

Don't accept the unacceptable.
Hugh Prather

SO THERE I WAS. In the end, one of the things I had most fervently wanted to prevent came to pass. Mama was left alone after a meal to gag and choke, and by the time anyone discovered her, she had aspirated and was gasping for breath. Now she was gone.

A recent exposé on central Indiana nursing homes included an investigation into the life-threatening hazards of improperly feeding elderly people who have impaired swallowing. My mother was not the only one to have succumbed in this manner, and the condition continues to be a significant cause of death among elderly people. I have learned that not only do elders sometimes noticeably choke and aspirate on the spot, they can also aspirate without anyone realizing it at the time. They can then develop a chronic and often terminal case of aspiration pneumonia. This casts a whole new light on all the coughing, wheezing, and respiratory treatments that characterized the last several months of my mother's life.

Mama's death freed me in one way. Since I no longer had to temper my criticism for fear of the consequences of speaking up, I was determined to see the chronic negligence I had witnessed at the nursing home come to light. I requested and received copies of Mama's chart records for the last few weeks of her life. I was stunned when the notes revealed a series of omissions. There were indeed no orders for my mother to receive extra fluids prior to the dehydration incident. In fact, I learned that Mama had been suffering from an upper respiratory infection just prior to the dehydration episode, and a drug given to treat the infection had a diuretic effect that made it a likely contributor to the subsequent dehydration. Gaps of more than a week appeared in the charts—even during the time when Mama had her G-tube removed. There was a last entry that, in its dishonesty, spoke volumes about what was happening in the facility. On the day of my mother's death, the final notation was at 1:30 P.M. Signed by the unit nurse, it stated that she had examined my mother and noted the details of her condition. This was an impossibility. Mama had passed on at precisely 1:21 P.M. Neither the unit nurse nor anyone else had been in the room since 10:30 that morning. The nurse who had come in after Mama died didn't appear until 3:00 P.M. At the very least, the charts proved that there were blatant discrepancies between what the staff did and what they said they did.

I hoped that these concrete examples would make officials dig deeper into the running of the facility. The letter I wrote to the Indiana State Department of Health was carefully worded, clearly and concisely focusing on the specific issues that I hoped they would address. I waited anxiously for news, hoping my letter would have some effect. Within a few weeks, the Department of Health concluded their investigation with the official pronouncement: No evidence of wrongdoing had been found. Yet a state regulator admitted to me—whether to comfort me or in her own frustration, I do not know— that she knew that all I had claimed and suspected was probably true. It is not very difficult for a nursing home to cover its tracks in such a situation. Unless someone on staff who knows what actually happened chooses to be a whistle-blower, the truth seldom comes out.

I pursued my effort to expose the treatment my mother received in the nursing home by contacting an attorney who specialized in elder care. I prepared a large packet of material for him to review. His reply to me— an explanation of why he declined to take the case—was discomfiting. While he believed that there was "negligence on the part of staff," he went on to say that because my mother was so old and so debilitated, and her care so difficult, there was really no case to be made. He seemed to be saying that under the circumstances, it didn't matter what had killed her. I was at a standstill.

I know only now about additional options I could have pursued. I was not aware at the time that I could have contacted a state ombudsman for long term care, who tracks complaints about nursing homes and who might have provided advice and guidance. Although nursing homes are supposed to post information about how to contact an ombudsman, I never saw any such notice where Mama resided. Nor did anyone on staff mention anything about it to me, including the social workers who were supposed to provide support to the family. I'm not sure what a discussion with an ombudsman might have yielded, but I would certainly have liked the opportunity to find out. I do not claim ignorance as an excuse, but it is important for other families of nursing home residents to be aware that they may find themselves becoming so overwhelmed and exhausted by their situations that they do not avail themselves of all the help that may be available.

Nowadays some nursing homes have family councils that act as both a source of support for families and a means to raise issues with a collective voice. When several families come together over similar problems, it reduces the chance that nursing home supervisors will isolate those who complain and thus will minimize their concerns. It has been my experience that there is seldom any naturally occurring contact between families of nursing home residents. However, the contact can be made, even for family members who live out of town, through such communication as e-mail and inexpensive long distance telephoning. I urge others to benefit from my hindsight and explore the family council as a potentially powerful option.

Nursing homes are a relatively recent fixture in our culture, which is part of the reason we are only just beginning to examine and take responsibility for them. With the advent of the Industrial Revolution and the resulting influx of people to the cities, it was not unusual for individuals or families to find themselves stranded without land or extended families to fall back on. By the turn of the century some immigrants and religious groups were running old folks' homes for their members, but many other aged people either were sent to mental institutions or wound up in poor houses. In 1935 concern for the rapidly increasing numbers of poor elderly along with a public outcry regarding conditions in poor houses led to a provision in the Social Security Act that barred anyone living in a poor house from receiving social security payments. The deliberate intention of this provision was to empty these blighted dwellings and encourage people to live either independently or in foster homes. To meet the subsequent rising need for housing for the elderly and to take advantage of this income opportunity, people who were strapped by the Depression and had few assets other than their homes began turning their residences into boarding houses for elderly people. In this way the first nursing homes came into being.

It wasn't long before facilities were built specifically as retirement or nursing homes, and with this came the move toward an institutional rather than a home setting for the care of elderly people. By the early 1950s public outcry about abuse and poor conditions once again precipitated change, leading to the first regulations governing nursing homes. Meanwhile, as the years went by, not only did the need for long term care facilities increase but so did the opportunities to make money from them. From real estate speculation to building contracts to revenue that could be collected on a per-bed basis, profits were there for the taking. Within a few decades homes for the aged had gone from poor houses to gold mines.

In the early 1970s several scandals, including the deaths of elders from fire in one facility and food poisoning in another, erupted into the public view. The nursing home system again came under national scrutiny. Led by passionate advocates, such as Senators Frank Moss and Claude Pepper, the Senate convened a Subcommittee on Aging, resulting in Congressional investigations and promises of reform. However, accounts from this era describe paltry attempts to prosecute wrongdoers, which allowed many nursing home operators to abscond with funds and remain unscathed. These nursing home operators were reputed to be politically influential. This, coupled with the fact that some politicians were investors in nursing homes themselves, handicapped far-reaching reform from the start.

(A few years ago a New Mexico magazine ran a series on the twenty-five wealthiest individuals in that state. I was stunned to discover that two of those wealthiest citizens had made their millions through ownership of nursing home chains. Surely there is something inherently, morally wrong about people becoming multi-millionaires by reaping their profits off the misery of the oldest, sickest, and most helpless of citizens. That article galvanized my intention to write about the disgrace of nursing homes through the eyes of someone who has been on the unprofitable end of them.)

Since the 1970s the federal government has managed to impose reams of regulations that often sound good on paper but, in practice, sometimes impede the delivery of quality care and divert attention from the real daily needs and interests of nursing home residents. Even where regulations appropriately mandate good care, lax enforcement can render them meaningless.

Billions of dollars in public funds continue to be poured into nursing homes. However, the way in which these funds are spent can create as many problems for the recipients of long term care as does a severe lack of funding. Nursing homes that are run for profit are much more likely to invest funds in what is perceived to increase profits and withhold funds from what is not so perceived, resulting in daily operations and delivery of care that suffer accordingly.

Two-thirds of the nearly 17,000 nursing homes now in operation in the United States are for-profit facilities, close to 85 percent of which are owned by chains. They are bought and sold on the open market, traded as commodities like anything else on the stock market. Mama's nursing home had started out being privately and locally owned, but as a parade of out-of-state corporate owners took over, conditions seemed to steadily deteriorate despite each new owner's glowing promises. With each proprietor came major staff changes, not only at the bottom rungs where turnover was already excessive but at the supervisory and administrative levels as well. I repeatedly had the experience of investing many hours in meetings, long distance telephone calls, and letters with administrators and supervising nurses only to return in a couple of months and find that none of them worked there anymore. So I would have to start over with a whole new crew.

The owners of the nursing home my mother was in kept the grounds perfectly manicured and placed expensive furnishings in the lobby. They ordered that the walls, which were free of noticeable marks or chipping and which looked fine, be painted even though there weren't enough linens—a fundamental necessity for providing basic care—to go around. Owners invest in appearances because that is what reels in new residents and their families, and hence increases revenues. When corporate financiers lay out a budget for bed and bath linens, they neglect to calculate the cost of intangibles, like the demoralization of nurse aides who cannot do their jobs because the day's supply of towels, washcloths, and sheets has run out. Nor do they appear to consider the social cost of the exodus of good staff, who become too discouraged and frustrated to continue. Evidence further suggests that they do not calculate the cost of the loss of comfort and dignity when a helpless elder must lie on dirty sheets, do without a top sheet or blanket, or even lie in his or her own waste because the meager supply of linens is used up faster than the laundry workers can replace them.

I would be remiss not to acknowledge that not all profit-based nursing homes are fueled by greed and disregard for the well-being of residents and staff. Some non-profit facilities have the same problems and short-comings as do their for-profit counterparts. The impoverished conditions of many nursing homes, when not a case of outright disregard, may be the result of lack of vision and sensitivity on the part of everyone from CEOs to the nursing home administrators who are in a position to make changes but who deny what is possible and turn their backs on the problems.

While the primary villains in shoddy nursing homes are proprietors who place profits above human beings, those who *should* be interceding on behalf of nursing home residents and staff have repeatedly dropped the ball. These are our state departments of health, whose job it is to enforce state and federal nursing home regulations. The disparate quality of nursing homes from state to state is a reflection of how vigorously each state's department of health is enacting and enforcing regulations. Nursing home advocates claim that in many states enforcement has been all but nonexistent, with little more than a written citation and no significant penalties for even the most grievous transgressions. In some states there have been accusations of high level corruption involving alliances between powerful state officials and nursing home operators.

Ultimately, the story of nursing homes in the United States is one of vested self-interests maintaining a system that gives short shrift to the people it serves and at the same time grossly exploits and misguides its employees. This is all sustained by a medical model philosophy that to a great extent disregards the real needs of nursing home residents. Surely, this is not what we want for our elders, nor is it what we want for those individuals who devote their lives to caring for our loved ones.

Despite this grim picture, I believe there may be a sea change occurring among some of America's corporate leaders as they become increasingly aware of the ultimate lack of fulfillment in the endless pursuit of money. These are people who are beginning to seek meaning in life not through how much wealth they can accumulate, but through how much they can give to the world. In addition, there are already some forward-thinking nursing home proprietors who are finding financially manageable ways to provide humane, high-quality services—services that benefit both residents and staff—without causing the economic disaster that many in the nursing home business self-servingly and short-sightedly predict.

18

HOPE RISING

The truth is that all human beings retain a capacity
for growth, no matter how small, until the last
breath is drawn.

Dr. William H. Thomas, Life Worth Living

DURING THE YEARS THAT my mother was in a
nursing home, I often fantasized about how it would be
if I were in control. I would begin by reallocating funds,
eliminating wasted time and money, and focusing on
issues that are of real value to both staff and residents. I
would revamp the current system to include nursing
home employees—nurses, nurse aides, social workers,
and so on—who are well educated, well trained, and well
paid. This would allow for these individuals to operate
under supportive circumstances that enable them to provide the dignified, compassionate, and skillful care that
our elders deserve.

To my fervent delight, I have discovered that an
increasing number of people all over the United States
are making this dream a reality. The nursing home
reform movement is gaining what I believe will prove to

be unstoppable momentum. Thanks to what was, at first, only a handful of visionaries, nursing homes scattered across the country are undergoing profound transformations. The people and facilities that are leading the way are showing that not only is it possible to deliver individualized, respectful care, but it also can be accomplished in an atmosphere that nurtures residents and employees alike. And the part that nursing home investors can relate to is that it doesn't have to cost a fortune to do so.

Within the nursing home reform movement, nursing home residents are not considered a problem to be solved. They are people at a particular stage in life whose needs should be the reason and purpose for all that goes on around them. Trying to force elders to adapt to the rigid, regimented, and demoralizing structure of a typical nursing home is absolutely backwards. It is the residents who should be at the center of nursing home reorganization. Across the board, nursing home reformers talk about the need for "culture change," the process of moving away from the medical model of nursing homes and toward people-centered enterprises that are fashioned after neighborhoods, which are then reintegrated into communities.

Several leaders in nursing home reform have come together to form a coalition under the name Pioneers in Nursing Home Culture Change. Many of these people began their crusades as a result of working in nursing homes themselves—as doctors, nurses, social workers, and administrators. They each have focused, in their own unique ways, on developing creative responses to the nursing home dilemma. Their action plans overlap and interweave into a rich tapestry that reflects the diverse elements needed for a new paradigm of providing care for elders in our society.

I first became aware of this quiet revolution when I read an article about a nursing home in upstate New York that was reported to be filled with potted plants, dogs, cats, birds, and children—and responsive elderly people redeemed from the ranks of the living dead. This model of transforming a hospital-like nursing home into a homelike one is known as the Eden Alternative. Dr. William H. Thomas, a Harvard-educated medical doctor with a special concern for the elderly, spearheads this process that has converted hundreds of nursing homes into human habitats. More and more facilities throughout the United States are becoming "Edenized" every year.

Naysayers who assume that such "radical" changes are impossible because of the expenses involved might be surprised to learn that this is not necessarily true. Because the Eden Alternative program promotes reorganizing staff away from a hierarchy model and into cooperative, self-empowered teams, studies have shown that staff turnover rates are greatly reduced at nursing homes in which the Eden Alternative is implemented. Overall use of medications needed for fighting infections has gone down. Also, residents have been documented as being less agitated, less irritable, and less depressed at these homes.

In other areas of the United States, Debora and Barry Barkan of California are working to alleviate the isolation felt by nursing home residents and to restore these elders' sense of value and connection to the rest of society. The Barkans recognize the need to organize a facility in a way that allows even the most withdrawn residents to participate in community life. Their Live Oak Regenerative Community is guided by the recognition that "the whole multigenerational community of the long term care environment is a sacred place in which love is the great healer. . . . Our expectation has been that each person—no matter how physically, mentally, or emotionally ravaged by disease she or he might be—has a place within that is healthy and that is capable of growth and development."

I have been made aware of other reformers who emphasize a holistic approach to how nursing homes are run. They eliminate rigid job descriptions so that staff are more broadly involved in all aspects of the nursing home, thus breaking down the walls of employee isolation as well as competition that can sometimes undermine the cooperation necessary for optimal functioning. Authority is also redirected by placing as much control as possible into the hands of residents.

Joanne Rader, a nurse, has been hard at work for many years finding ways to redirect nursing home resources, specifically to help reduce the use of restraints and to individualize the care of nursing home residents. Her work has been aimed at "teaching staff how to be creative and compassionate when addressing behavioral symptoms related to dementia, and to see that persons with dementia still retain the right to direct their own care." A primary principle in the accomplishment of her goal is for staff to be willing to modify a resident's environment in order to best suit the resident, rather than expecting the resident to modify herself to accommodate the facility.

Ms. Rader tells a wonderful story about an elderly woman who did not sleep well in her bed. This resident also presented a number of other issues, including a tendency to behave aggressively toward others. Then the staff found that the woman was most happy when sitting in her wheelchair behind the nurses station. Because this also meant less trouble for the staff, they made the necessary alterations in that area to make it safe and convenient for the woman to be there. Once the woman grew drowsy, though, she would slowly slide out of her chair and into the space beneath the desk, where she would continue to sleep soundly. To my amazement, instead of hauling her out of there, the nurses got the woman a mattress, pillow, and linens to make a comfortable bed underneath the desk. They even took the trouble to explain this novel approach to visitors who noticed. Meanwhile, this elderly woman had finally found a place to sleep where she apparently felt contented and secure. Not only did she sleep well for the rest of her life, but she grew less anxious and opened up in ways that had been unseen prior to that unique arrangement. The staff of this nursing home had helped this aged woman to live and die in peace.

I have visited one nursing home that has embraced the concept of reducing the use of physical and chemical restraints by means of individualizing resident care.

Within a few years this facility has gone from restraining sixty to seventy percent of its residents down to zero percent. The director of nursing attributes this accomplishment to scrutinizing the circumstances of each person and finding an alternative solution to whatever it was that led to restraints in the first place. Simple strategies worked for many residents, such as different seating accommodations and lowering beds nearer the floor so residents were less prone to injury when trying to get out.

That particular nursing home has much to be proud of in the strides it has made. Their success was reflected by both the general atmosphere within the home and by the appearance and demeanor of the residents. Even though nearly the entire population of this facility consisted of total care residents, the residents I saw all appeared alert—they looked at me, and most exchanged greetings. No one was calling out for help. On the less positive side, this facility was still housed in a medical-style building on a busy street in a commercial neighborhood. Pictures that had been hung in corridors did little to alter the institutional atmosphere, and all the aides were dressed in clinical white. I was left feeling that there was still a long way to go but that meaningful change had occurred.

Naomi Feil, a geriatric social worker based in Cleveland, has devoted a lifetime's professional effort to developing a system that enables elders to make peace with any unresolved issues they may have in their lives. Her groundbreaking method is aptly called Validation and constitutes a breakthrough in the psychological care of elders. A combination of genuinely wanting to help the elderly people in her care along with being willing to look through the eyes of elders has enabled Ms. Feil to see meaning where others had seen only nonsense.

She explains that "[w]hen their eyes fail and the outside world blurs, very old people look inside. They use their vivid mind's eye to see. People from the past become real. When recent memory goes and time blurs, very old people begin to measure life in terms of memories, not minutes. When the very old lose their speech, similar sounds, rhythms, and early learned movements substitute for words. To survive the present-day losses, the very old restore the past. They find much wisdom in the past."

People who interact with mentally disabled elders based on this philosophy are able not only to help many of them resolve issues from their pasts but also to interrupt their march into greater isolation. Validation techniques can aid in reversing communication breakdowns as well as reestablish a significant degree of the ability to participate in one's present surroundings. To bring any measure of peace and resolution to someone in their eleventh hour, someone whom society has often abandoned to the rudiments of custodial care, is no small feat and is to be applauded.

Ms. Feil writes that she "learned that very old disoriented people have an intuitive wisdom, a basic humanity that we all share. Behind their disorientation lies a human knowing. This humanity stretches beyond present ties, culture, race, geography, and religion. When present time and place fade, when work goes, when rules no longer matter, when social obligations have lost meaning, a basic humanity shines through."

Ms. Feil tells the story of a woman who was planning to stop visiting her mother in a nursing home because the woman was so distressed by what she perceived as her mother's incessant ramblings and apparent lack of recognition of her daughter's identity. A nurse trained in Validation was able to step in and demonstrate for this daughter a means to enter into her mother's world. The grateful daughter was then dissuaded from abandoning her mother once she was able to find meaning in her mother's utterances as well as to participate in assisting her in resolving the issues they reflected.

The techniques of Validation are within the reach of anyone who wants to be trained in them, and once learned they take only a few minutes per day to implement. The time and energy that is saved in dealing with a person's problems and upsets can more than offset the cost of training and time spent engaged in the process. While the Validation method is in widespread use in nursing homes in Europe and Australia, it has been slower to catch on in the United States. Here, the medical model, and funding sources oriented to it, have focused on treatments that are aimed at reality orientation—remembering the trivia of daily life. Just as I learned from spending time with my mother, Ms. Feil points out that most disoriented elders are disinterested in such information, and retrieving it does absolutely nothing to ameliorate their difficulties.

I am heartened and inspired to have discovered

that the numbers of these wonderful reformers are growing all over the United States, and they share a common vision for how the incapacitated elderly should be cared for, what nursing homes can be, and how to bring that vision into reality. What once seemed like a daunting project with overwhelming, if not insurmountable, obstacles is proving to be not only possible but also eventually within reach of every nursing home in America. Much work still needs to be done, but the fact that it has *begun* means a great deal.

Leaders who strive to change nursing homes make the point that reform is not something that can be done overnight. Instead, it is an ongoing, living process that requires constant responsiveness and alterations. Nursing home reform is clearly not about simply redecorating and bringing in a few pets and plants. It is about a profound transformation in how we view the disabled elderly and those who care for them. It is about a major reorganization of facilities and personnel, continually being adjusted as more is learned about how to do things even better.

A holistic philosophy that takes all aspects of providing care for our oldest citizens into account is the best and most appropriate approach. However, it is also important to work with each nursing home based on where things currently stand there, which often means making small changes in one specific area at a time. It is difficult for people to learn to do things differently from how they have always done them. Sometimes it is difficult even to admit that there might be a better way. Taking things one step at a time can ease that opposition.

Using chemical restraints in nursing homes is another major problem that is being addressed by all of those behind the reform movement. Granted, entire populations of nursing homes are seldom tranquilized en masse to the point of insensibility as they once were in some places, but psychotropic medications are still widely given to residents as behavioral controls. Dr. Thomas, creator of the Eden Alternative, points out in *Life Worth Living* how unnecessary this practice can be:

> We would all be outraged at a health facility that placed its residents in darkened rooms and then prescribed medications to improve their vision. Common sense tells us that these people need light, not drugs. When we place frail, demented, elderly people in long-term care facilities and shut them away from companionship, usefulness, and variety in their daily lives, we, too, create a "need" for medications. In this case, major and minor tranquilizers are the drugs of choice. While there are some nursing home residents who truly need and benefit from such medications, the bulk of these drugs are used to compensate for the failings of the institution.

Nursing homes that embark on a reform process find that they are able to eliminate the use of psychotropic medications for many residents merely by making sure the residents have frequent opportunities for social interaction. Something as simple as teaching aides to make eye contact with residents while they speak to them and while they minister to their physical needs has made a huge difference. Residents who are taken off antipsychotic drugs and put on antidepressants suffer fewer side effects and are no longer reduced to a stupor.

Reform-minded nursing homes also will no doubt increasingly see the value of supporting and encouraging relationships among residents. Roommates' chairs can be placed facing one another for a while each day so that they can see each other. A staff person can later act as an intermediary to let each person know a little bit about the other, about interests, life experiences, or things they may have had in common over their lives. Even with residents whose communication abilities are impaired, a sense of connectedness can be fostered. As has been discovered with aviaries placed in common areas, this focus of attention on something in the elders' midst has a potentially stimulating effect. After a while, extended connections and variety can be provided by bringing familiar pairs together with other pairs. Staff will need to be trained to be aware of both affection and aversion, making allowances for closeness and distance accordingly. Encouraging this kind of familiarity and fellowship can go a long way toward alleviating the isolation that so many institutionalized disabled elders feel.

Another nursing home I have visited recently is in the process of embarking on the Eden Alternative model. They were guided by the fundamental concept that all their residents, no matter how impaired, needed to be given the opportunity to feel that they had a purpose. By following that intention, ingenious methods had been devised to engage people in a variety of activities. One woman, who busied herself with repetitive picking motions, was given the job of removing loose threads from rag strips that were to be used for rug making. Instead of sitting in isolation picking at nothing for hours on end, she became a functioning part of a group. Those who are not able to participate in any overt activities are given massage therapy and the opportunity to listen to music. The sounds of birds singing and chirping added a delightful backdrop to the atmosphere.

In both facilities I visited that were embracing reform, I was struck by the fact that there were no voices calling out, no rows of geri-chairs lined up anywhere. Everyone seemed to be someplace in particular, and there was a feeling of calm and orderliness. I was deeply touched to see how much of a difference even the beginnings of reform could make. Both facilities reported an emphasis on taking better care of their staff as well, including such things as providing free massage and other on-site, stress-reducing modalities.

One of the biggest misconceptions that must be overcome concerning our elders is believing that anyone is beyond help. This belief is common and can be found among government regulators, doctors, nursing home personnel, families of the elderly, and the general public. According to Robin Marantz Henig, who has written about the mismanagement of elderly mental health issues in *The Myth of Senility*,

> ... the silver lining in this story is that, while
> old people are particularly vulnerable to environ-

mental stresses, they are also particularly responsive
to environmental supports. Old brains are remarkably pliable, capable of springing back to life—in
terms of both revived personalities and actual
regenerated brain cells—if conditions are ripe. This
fact adds a poignant urgency to the growing cry
that the elderly deserve an honored place in
Western society. To deny them that place is to deny
them the opportunity not only to maintain their
mental functioning but also to grow.

How can we continue to abandon our elders to
boredom, loneliness, and loss of hope and purpose?
Every nursing home must adopt as its governing principle the recognition that *total care* means care of the
entire human being—physically, psychologically, emotionally, and spiritually. The dependent elderly must
be reintegrated into society, such that nursing homes
become thriving, lively places that are part of the community and not remain sterile, uninviting buildings that
essentially isolate the oldest and sickest from sight.
Nursing homes do not have to be places that family
members dread stepping into and can hardly wait to
escape; they can be places with warm, nurturing
ambiances where people in the midst of their busy, fast-
paced lives can relax and rejuvenate in the company of
their loved ones. It is happening today in cities and
towns all over America—maybe in your own neighborhood. Look and see. If it isn't happening in your neighborhood yet, ask why not.

While reformers consider motivated, dedicated

leaders, known as "change makers," to be essential, they also know that for nursing home reform to succeed, there must be a team effort involving everyone from government regulators and nursing home operators to the nursing home administrators and the medical, kitchen, laundry, and maintenance personnel. Nursing homes can and should become places where people look forward to doing their jobs, where people feel empowered and inspired, and where people are paid wages that allow them to take good care of themselves and their families.

And, of course, to make sweeping changes work, nursing home reform requires residents themselves to be involved, with the support, understanding, and cooperation of their families. By and large it is the residents who offer the quickest and most positive responses when reform has occurred, validating the success of everyone's efforts.

The acceptance and support of the community for making changes in the nursing home system is vital as well, and that means it ultimately requires all of us to participate. As most people will agree, change does not come easily, even when we all want it and know that the end result will be a good one. Nursing home reformers run into resistance at all levels—regulatory, proprietary, funding, medical, administrative, staff, families of the residents, etc. Still, reformers are able to prove time and again that once people understand the purpose behind the reform and are given an opportunity to experience what it would be like, they most often embrace it wholeheartedly. Supporting the individuals who are making valiant efforts to bring about change is critical. We need to do our parts to keep them hanging in there until the tide turns.

Only by facing the truth head on about the American nursing home system can we hope to help those who are trapped in it—the residents, their families, and the employees. By 2030 it is expected that 20 percent of the population in the United States, or 69 million people, will be over 65 years old. More than half of all nursing home residents will be suffering from some degree of cognitive impairment.

Today, more than 75 percent of nursing home reimbursements, totaling billions of dollars per year, come from United States taxpayers in the form of Medicare and Medicaid. It is our money, and we must insist that it be spent well. Contrary to industry claims, wide-ranging reform measures implemented to improve the quality of care and the quality of life of nursing home residents, while improving employee well-being at the same time, actually result in significant reductions in costs in many areas. We are often misled into believing that doing things well is too expensive. It is not too expensive, however, when funds already allotted are redirected appropriately.

In the long run, the only way that sweeping reform will succeed in nursing homes is if enough people demand it, demand whatever it takes to bring about a real transformation. Until nursing home employees are paid competitive wages that will attract more talented people to the work, until nursing home owners and managers are committed to making the quality of the service they provide a priority, and until legislators pass legislation that ensures excellent care and see to it that it is enforced, the struggle for nursing home reform will remain an uphill battle.

As things stand now, nursing homes that reflect the new paradigm in long-term care are very much in the minority. Yet, day by day, this is changing. Each nursing home that turns itself around touches more lives than just its employees, residents, and residents' families. Each one shines as a beacon to others, demonstrating what is possible. When enough people see what true total care looks like, they will no longer accept the mediocre impostor that now prevails in American nursing homes.

As the nursing home reform movement continues to gain momentum, not only do we have the addition of hundreds of facilities embarking on this all-out change, but we also begin to see hints of change appearing in nursing homes that are still operating along traditional lines. Staff in key positions are becoming increasingly sensitive to and aware of the psychological and emotional needs of the residents, and aware of the need for their staff to be more humane and considerate toward their charges. This may even be seen as a reflection of the gradual maturing of our culture and of the growing recognition of how valuable compassion is and what it means to implement it.

In the meantime, it is up to each of us to open our eyes and hearts to the shameful plight of our dependent elders, and to commit ourselves to the idea that nursing homes do not have to be the way most are now. It can be overwhelming to think of reforming something as huge and complex as the American nursing home system— there is no question that it is a massive and multifaceted endeavor—but it becomes manageable when one nursing home at a time, one issue at a time, is addressed. This is how it is being done, and this is how it is working.

I believe that someday I will have the comfort of knowing that no dependent elder and no loved one of a dependent elder will ever again have to endure what my mother and family did. I will celebrate the day when I can look around and see that nursing homes are truly places where the phases of life are respected and where people's dignity is honored. When the nursing home becomes a healthy and functional communal living arrangement for our elders, with appreciated caregivers watching over them, we will remember that the root of *nursing* means "nurturing," and we will know that the *home* part is finally true.

Appendix A

Selecting a nursing home for your loved one

♦ Make inquires among people in the community who have relatives in nursing homes to get preliminary recommendations about those facilities.

♦ Call your state ombudsman to find out how to obtain copies of inspection reports on the facilities you are considering.

♦ Find out if the facility has a waiting list. If it does, this can be a good sign about the quality of care offered. In case this is the facility you finally choose, you should add your loved one's name to the list right away.

♦ When you visit the facilities you are considering, visit more than once, and visit at least one time without notifying them you are coming. Mornings are the busiest hours in nursing homes and are a good time to evaluate how well the facility is run. Weekends, on the other hand, are when most facilities are at their worst, so they are a good time to visit as well.

◆ Be sure one of your visits is during a meal time. Notice whether residents who are being fed are paid attention and are fed considerately. Try to determine whether the food looks and smells appetizing. Ask if you can view the kitchen so you can evaluate how clean it is and how orderly the meal preparation procedures are. Ask to see some sample menus as well.

◆ Look closely at the residents and observe whether they appear clean, comfortably positioned, and alert. (If a lot of them look "out of it," this could be a red flag for widespread use of chemical restraints.)

◆ Be cognizant of whether physical restraints are in use.

◆ Are nonambulatory residents engaged in something, or are they just parked somewhere? How many people are up as opposed to being in bed?

◆ Ask specific questions relevant to the condition of your loved one, such as what activities he or she could be included in.

◆ Find out how many staff members are devoted to recreational and therapeutic activities—i.e., massage therapists, activity directors, music therapists, etc.

◆ Ask what sort of community involvement occurs. Is there a pet therapy program? Do they have programs in which children visit regularly?

◆ Pay attention to how the facility feels to you. Does the atmosphere seem chaotic and the staff rushed? Or is there an air of calm and efficiency?

◆ Scrutinize what is transpiring around you. Do you see aides and nurses speaking to the residents? Or does the staff seem to be going about their business with few interactions?

◆ Ask whether families are encouraged to participate in their loved one's care and whether a family council exists. If there is a family council, ask how often it meets and how many people participate.

◆ Try to seek out family members of current residents to ask them about the facility. People seem more willing to open up if you give them your phone number or approach them outside in the parking lot than if you try to talk with them inside the facility.

◆ Above all else, don't deny your doubts—address them.

APPENDIX B

Working with a family council

◆ One important avenue often available to families to help them advocate for their loved ones in nursing homes is the family council. By joining with others, family members are able to speak with a collective voice and feel a greater sense of empowerment when addressing issues with a facility. These support groups can also provide emotional support and encouragement when situations seem overwhelming or when families aren't sure how to proceed with their loved ones' care.

◆ Since family councils do not have to be limited only to families associated with one specific nursing home, this resource is particularly important for those who do not live in the city in which their loved one is institutionalized. Connecting with families who have loved ones in different facilities can also provide a perspective by way of comparison.

◆ In addition, family councils can team up with other support groups to bring in speakers and trainers who can assist them in a variety of ways. Families can learn more about what to expect from a nursing home and how to deal with a particular facility or certain issues more effectively. Groups can also bring in experienced educators who can provide them with the understanding and skills to relate to their loved ones in the various stages that the elders may be going through.

◆ If at all possible, don't try to go it alone. Look for help wherever you can.

BIBLIOGRAPHY

Armstrong, April Oursler. *Cry Babel: The Nightmare of Aphasia and a Courageous Woman's Struggle to Rebuild Her Life.* Garden City, NY: Doubleday, 1979.

Bergquist, William H., Rod McLean, and Barbara A. Kobylinski. *Stroke Survivors.* San Francisco: Jossey-Bass Publishers, 1994.

Bauby, Jean-Dominique. *The Diving Bell and the Butterfly: A Memoir of Life in Death.* New York: Vintage Books, 1998.

Broida, Helen. *Coping with Stroke: Communication Breakdown of Brain Injured Adults.* Houston: College-Hill Press, 1979.

Budish, Armond D. *Avoiding the Medicaid Trap: How to Beat the Catastrophic Costs of Nursing-Home Care.* New York: Henry Holt & Co., 1989.

Chödrön, Pema. *The Wisdom of No Escape: And the Path of Loving-Kindness.* Boston: Shambhala Publications, Inc., 1991.

Fagan, Rose Marie, Carter Cartlett Williams, and Sarah Greene Burger. Final report of the meeting of Pioneers in Nursing Home Culture Change, October 1997. (For copies, contact Rose Marie Fagan at LIFESPAN of Greater Rochester, (716) 454-3224, ext. 115.)

Feil, Naomi. *The Validation Breakthrough: Simple Techniques for Communicating with People with "Alzheimer's-Type Dementia."* 3rd ed. Baltimore: Health Professions Press, 1995.

Freese, Arthur S. *Stroke: The New Hope and the New Help.* New York: Random House, 1980.

Gardner, Howard. *The Shattered Mind: The Person after Brain Damage.* New York: Alfred A. Knopf, 1974.

Gordon, Harley. *How to Protect Your Life Savings from Catastrophic Illness and Nursing Homes: A Handbook for Financial Survival.* Boston: Financial Planning Institute, 1990.

Henig, Robin Marantz. *The Myth of Senility: Misconceptions about the Brain and Aging.* Garden City, NY: Anchor Press/Doubleday, 1981.

Hillman, James. *The Force of Character: And the Lasting Life.* New York: Random House, 1999.

Hughes, Marylou. *The Nursing Home Experience: A Family Guide to Making It Better.* New York: The Crossroad Publishing Co., Inc., 1992.

Ilardo, Joseph A. *As Parents Age: A Psychological and Practical Guide.* Acton, MA: VanderWyk & Burnham, 1998.

Kübler-Ross, Elisabeth. *The Wheel of Life: A Memoir of Living and Dying.* New York: Scribner, 1997.

Laird, Carobeth. *Limbo: A Memoir about Life in a Nursing Home by a Survivor.* Novato, CA: Chandler & Sharp Publishers, Inc., 1979.

Larsen, Dorothy. *A Touch of Sage: Reflections on Growth, Change, and Growing Older.* Minneapolis: CompCare Publishers, 1989.

Mace, Nancy L., and Peter V. Rabins. *The 36-Hour Day: A Family Guide to Caring for Persons with Alzheimer's Disease, Related Dementing Illnesses, and Memory Loss in Later Life.* Baltimore: Johns Hopkins University Press, 1999.

Masson, Jeffrey Moussaieff. *Dogs Never Lie about Love: Reflections on the Emotional World of Dogs.* New York: Crown Publishers, 1997.

Mindell, Arnold. *Coma: Key to Awakening.* Boston: Shambhala Publications, Inc., 1989.

Moss, Frank E., and Val J. Halamandaris. *Too Old, Too Sick, Too Bad: Nursing Homes in America.* Germantown, MD: Aspen Systems Corp., 1977.

Nuland, Sherwin B. *How We Die: Reflections on Life's Final Chapter.* New York: Alfred A. Knopf, 1994.

Ornstein, Robert. *The Roots of the Self: Unraveling the Mystery of Who We Are.* San Francisco: HarperSanFrancisco, 1993.

Ram Dass. *Still Here: Embracing Aging, Changing, and Dying.* New York: The Putnam Publishing Group, 2000.

Rollins, Mary Richards. *Patients, Pain, and Politics: Nursing Home Inspector's Shocking True Story and Expert Advice for You and Your Family.* Fountain Valley, CA: New Century Publishing, 1994.

Safford, Florence. *Caring for the Mentally Impaired Elderly: A Family Guide.* New York: Henry Holt & Co., 1986.

Smith, Genevieve Waples. *Care of the Patient with a Stroke: A Handbook for the Patient's Family and the Nurse.* New York: Springer Publishing Co., 1976.

Thomas, William H. *Life Worth Living: How Someone You Love Can Still Enjoy Life in a Nursing Home—The Eden Alternative in Action.* Acton, MA: VanderWyk & Burnham, 1996.

Vladeck, Bruce C. *Unloving Care: The Nursing Home Tragedy.* New York: Basic Books, 1980.

Wright, H. T. *The Matthew Tree.* New York: Pantheon Books, 1975.

RESOURCES

Alzheimer's Association
919 North Michigan Avenue
Chicago, IL 60611-1676
Phone: (800) 272-3900
Fax: (312) 335-1110
E-mail: info@alz.org
Website: www.alz.org

American Health Care
  Association
1201 L Street NW
Washington, DC 20005
Phone: (202) 842-4444
Fax: (202) 842-3860
Website: www.ahca.org

The Eden Alternative™
742 Turnpike Road
Sherburne, NY 13460
Phone: (607) 674-5232
Fax: (607) 674-6723
E-mail: info@edenalt.com
Website: www.edenalt.com

Hospice Foundation of
  America
2001 S Street NW, Suite 300
Washington, DC 20009

Phone: (800) 854-3402
Fax: (202) 638-5312
E-mail:
hfa@hospicefoundation.org
Website:
www.hospicefoundation.org

Institute for Quality
  Improvement in Long
  Term Health Care
Southwest Texas State
  University
601 University Drive
San Marcos, TX 78666
Phone: (512) 245-8234
Fax: (512) 245-7803
Website:
www.health.swt.edu/ltci/ltci.html

Long Term Care Campaign
P.O. Box 27394
Washington, DC 20038
Phone: (202) 434-3744
Fax: (202) 434-6403
E-mail:
info@ltccampaign.org
Website:
www.ltccampaign.org

National Citizens' Coalition
for Nursing Home Reform
1424 16th Street NW,
Suite 202
Washington, DC 20036-
2211
Phone: (202) 332-2275
Fax: (202) 332-2949
E-mail: nccnhr@nccnhr.org
Website: www.nccnhr.org

National Hospice and
Palliative Care
Organization
1700 Diagonal Road,
Suite 300
Alexandria, VA 22314

Phone: (703) 243-5900
Fax: (703) 525-5762
E-mail:
webmaster@nhpco.org
Website: www.nhpco.org

Validation® Training
Institute
21987 Byron Road
Cleveland, OH 44122
Phone: (216) 561-0357
or (216) 881-0040
Fax: (216) 751-6434
E-mail:
naomifeil@aol.com
Website:
www.vfvalidation.org

INDEX

OCT 26 2000
0 4 DEC 2000